HEART OF ENGLAND

WALKS FOR MOTORISTS

Richard Shurey

30 Walks with sketch maps

COUNTRYSIDE BOOKS
NEWBURY, BERKSHIRE

*Countryside Books' walking guides cover most areas of England and
Wales and include the following series:*

County Rambles
Walks For Motorists
Exploring Long Distance Paths
Literary Walks
Pub Walks

A complete list is available from the publishers

First Published 1977
by Frederick Warne Ltd

This completely revised and updated edition
published 1992

© Richard Shurey 1992

COUNTRYSIDE BOOKS
3 Catherine Road
Newbury, Berkshire

ISBN 1 85306 166 2

Cover photograph: Kenilworth Castle taken by Bill Meadows

Publishers' Note
At the time of publication all footpaths used in these walks were
designated as official footpaths or rights of way, but it should be borne in
mind that diversion orders may be made from time to time.
Although every care has been taken in the preparation of this Guide,
neither the Author nor the Publisher can accept responsibility for those
who stray from the Rights of Way.

Produced through MRM Associates Ltd., Reading
Typeset by Wessex Press Design & Print Limited, Warminster
Printed in England by J. W. Arrowsmith Ltd., Bristol

Contents

Introduction

How often have you seen a rather forlorn-looking footpath sign pointing a way over the countryside and wondered what was on the other side of the stile?

The Midland counties have some of the highest densities of footpaths in the land — Worcestershire boasts 4½ miles to the square mile. These rights of way are in danger of extinction; there is little point in retaining a track if it is not used but, if they disappear, part of the heritage of our land would be destroyed at the same time.

The network of pathways was evolved over many centuries; one route was perhaps the way to the church, another the track leading from a farmstead to an inn or a village. They became established by common usage.

All the walks start and finish at the same place. Where names of places for refreshment are mentioned they are included only as a guide — they are not paid advertisements.

I have described, as accurately as possible, the rights of way as indicated on the latest Ordnance Survey maps and the Definitive Maps held by the County Councils. If I have erred and encouraged you to trespass — my apologies!

Although on a designated footpath one has the legal right of unhindered passage, one should treat this as a privilege — a privilege which should not be abused. The Country Code should be followed:

1. Guard against fire risk.
2. Fasten all gates.
3. Keep dogs under proper control.
4. Keep to the paths across farmland.
5. Avoid damaging fences, hedges and walls.
6. Leave no litter.
7. Safeguard water supplies.
8. Protect wild life, wild plants and trees.
9. Go carefully on country roads.
10. Respect the life of the countryside.

A map is not strictly necessary if this guide is carried as the routes are described in detail and sketch-maps provided. An Ordnance Survey map, however, adds interest and helps identify points in distant prospects that are not mentioned. The sheet number of the appropriate 1:50,000 O.S. map is quoted at the beginning of each walk in the guide and map references are given in the text to assist map reading. The first two numerals refer to the number of the grid line (recorded along the top and bottom margins of the map) to the left of the place on the map. The third numeral is the estimated tenth eastwards to the next grid line. Similarly, the next two numerals are the number of the grid line (recorded on the side margins of the map) below the situation of the place on the map. The last numeral is the estimated tenth northwards to the next grid line.

'I nauseate walking; it is a country diversion. I loathe the country,' wrote Congreve. Doubtless, life was calmer in those far-off days. Today the main highways are a maelstrom and a ramble along some of our lovely green pathways is an antidote to the hectic pressures of life. I prefer the sentiments of Christina Rossetti to those of Congreve:

> Before green apples blush,
> Before green nuts embrown,
> Why, one day in the country
> Is worth a month in town.

So pack that map, pull on the boots or shoes and come 'over the hills and far away'.

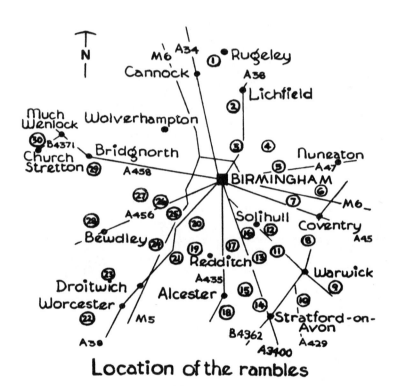

Location of the rambles

CASTLE RING, CANNOCK CHASE

WALK 1

★

5 miles (8 km)

OS Landranger 128

Surrounded as it is by so much industrial despoliation, it is surprising that Cannock Chase retains so much wild grandeur. It now covers 26 square miles, is roamed by herds of fallow deer and was designated in 1958 an Area of Outstanding Natural Beauty.

The region escaped much enclosure as the soil is gravelly and was considered too poor for agriculture. It did support a type of grey-faced sheep peculiar to the Chase and Cannock was a thriving market town for their sale. The Chase was, from Norman times, a favourite hunting ground.

The loftiest point of the woodlands which now cover Cannock Chase, is just over 800 ft above sea level at Castle Ring.

A five-sided hill fort is situated on the plateau. The earthworks, constructed by the early Britons about 2,000 years ago, were probably used as a place of refuge when invaders advanced up the valley of the Trent. The fortification is extensive and a huge population could have been accommodated.

A car park will be found at Castle Ring and an inn is close at hand, so this makes a good place to park and start a five-mile walk through the forest glades of the Chase.

After exploring the ridges and ditches of the fort, take the sign-posted pathway beside a sweet-smelling wood of pine and birch trees (Map 128/045127). Follow the 'Heart of England' way sign and keep the fort and the trig. plinth on your right. Cross a wide track, and enter the forestlands. We soon rejoin the main forest 'road' and the way can be seen far ahead, carving a clear way over the undulating countryside. There is a fine contrast of blues and greens with plantations of Scots and Corsican pines.

The route goes past timbers (are pit props still of wood?) reminding us that, beautiful though it is, this is essentially a working forest. A tiny stream, where children love to dash through the water, is crossed, and the track then climbs to a road (039143). Turn right. At a road junction, a stony way (Marquis Drive) goes left. This can be used by vehicles, so after 400 yards take a shady path on the right through a barrier. (The track takes

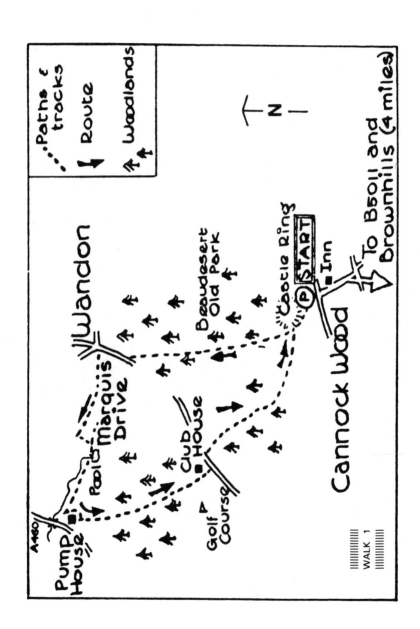

Paths & tracks
Route
Woodlands

— N —

Wandon

Beaudesert Old Park

Pool Marquis Drive

Club House

Golf Course

Pump House

A460

Castle Ring

START

P

■ Inn

To Broil and Brownhills (4 miles)

Cannock Wood

WALK 1

8

its name from a carriage road of the Marquis of Anglesey who once owned the great estate of Beaudesert.)

The track borders a nursery of trees and passes huge beeches. When a T-junction is reached, proceed left to rejoin Marquis Drive. Our way to the right passes a lovely mere and goes beside a meandering stream.

Just before a road (the A460), go past a vehicle barrier to the left. Beyond this the track goes uphill (a new pumping station is on your right), then veers around to the right. At a house there is an assortment of tracks; our way is over the crest of the hill. Attractive views now open up over the Chase and the Trent Valley — a good excuse to 'stand and stare'.

Further on, stand and stare again — this time to look for flying golf balls before crossing a golf course to a road. Turn left to a place opposite the drive to the clubhouse (029136). Here you will see a green track on the right running parallel to the road.

After about 400 yards, by a vehicle barrier, walk sharp right, away from the road. This is another lovely track, high above the lake of Beaudesert Old Park. On the right, a colliery wheel is soon seen for we are walking over the rich Cannock coal seams. At a crossing of tracks, walk straight over and climb the steep slopes back to Castle Ring.

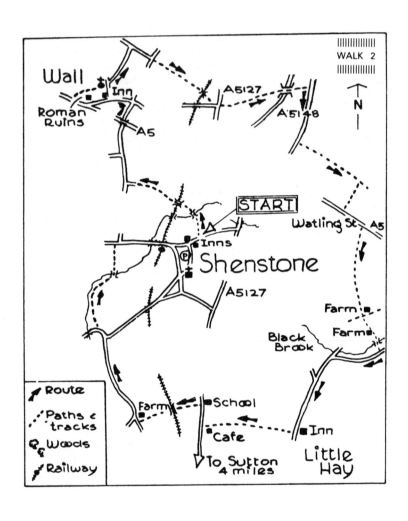

SHENSTONE AND ROMAN WALL

★

8½ miles (13.5 km)

OS Landranger 139

In Roman times, Levocetum was a thriving town; its importance as a posting station was increased by being at the junction of the two great highways of Watling Street and Icknield Street.

Today, this same place is Wall, a hamlet some three miles from Lichfield. The ruins of Levocetum have been carefully excavated and the elaborate bathhouse is especially interesting. There is a little museum housing some of the finds.

This ramble starts from Shenstone, a growing residential and industrial village where the prominent church tower is a dominating landmark.

There are several quiet streets in Shenstone, suitable for parking. From the war memorial, walk past two inns — the Railway and the Plough and Harrow. A few yards further, on the left, is a signposted footpath (Map 139/109048) and then, after a stile, is a pleasant field path which crosses a twisting brook. Ahead now is a bridge over a railway. The vehicle track soon disappears and the footpath continues on the same heading over a field to a farm drive, then goes left to a lane.

Our way is to the right, along Ashcroft Lane. Go by farmsteads to pass under the A5 road to a crossroads. To the left is the Trooper inn and the site of the Roman township. The ghosts of the legionaries are surely lurking hereabouts! By the telephone box and 'No Through Road' sign there is a footpath towards the spire of Wall church. On a lane, proceed to the right and a lane (signposted Lichfield) then takes us left (099067).

At a T-junction, proceed to the right and cross a road. The vehicle way is marked as a private road for motors but is a right of way for walkers. Away to the left are the three pencil-like spires of Lichfield Cathedral. The track goes over bracing countryside and under a railway bridge to a lane. A yard or so to the left is the main A5127 road. Straight across is another farm track.

The route follows the footpath to cross a dual carriageway to a farmstead. Continue to a lane. Turn right for ½ mile then turn left through a gateway and along a wide bridleway. The way is marked on large-scale maps as Swifen Lane and it would seem that the road makers had little use for this ancient track.

Opposite a gate, and by a large dead tree, go right, through a gap in the hedge. An undefined track takes us to Watling Street (126052). Turn left and stay on the busy road until you see, by farm cottages, a footpath notice which indicates the way to Weeford and Manley. Keep at the edge of a field to a stile, then stay on the same heading to a wide track. We go by woodlands and a farm called Thickbroom. Go over a crossing track and by another farmhouse.

An attractive drive bordered by weeping willows goes over Black Brook — a misnomer as it looks like silver on a sunny day — and, on reaching a lane, our way is right. Keep not far from the tumbling waters of the stream for some way and then the winding lane bears left to The Holly Bush inn.

On the other side of the lane is the start of a field path (123028). Keep by the hedge to a stile; the hedge should then be on your left in a meadow. An oft-walked pathway now brings us to the A38. Continue to the right. Near a school, leave the road and walk along a public footpath on the left. The track goes under a railway and across fields to a latchgate by henhouses and we emerge on a lane to the left of cottages.

Turn right. Just past Footherley Hall we join the route of Icknield Street. Go straight ahead at the junction reached after about half a mile. Within a few yards is a footpath sign on the right. Bearing round to the left, keep by the woods where bluebells bloom, to a fast brook. Turn right to the bridge where the water is crossed. The track now goes by an industrial site to a lane to Shenstone and two friendly inns.

SUTTON PARK

The Park of Sutton Coldfield has been described as a miniature Dartmoor and certainly, by the strict terms of the famous Royal Charter and diligent guardianship, it has remained a rare example of English countryside virtually unchanged for many hundreds of years. But why 'Coldfield', and how was the solitude disturbed by a railway straight across the middle of the Chase? But we are leaping ahead!

The ancient Britons roamed over the area. Maney, an oft-used place name, comes from the Anglo-Saxon 'meini' — the stones. There are several tumuli, encampments and dykes in and about the Park. The Romans left their significant mark — the mile and a half of Icknield Street. It is one of the least disturbed sections of Roman highway in Britain and leaves the Park at Streetly, the field on the Street.

In the dark Mercian days, when the area was part of a great chase for hunting, a lodge, called Southtun, was built on Maney Hill on the edge of the Coldfield (ie the field on the hill). So the town of Sutton Coldfield was born.

After the Normans divided the country, the Domesday Book recorded the woods of Sutton and valued them at four pounds. Above Wyndley Pool there was a spacious Norman manor house, the lines of which could still be traced in contemporary records only a hundred years ago. Sutton market was established early in the 14th century by Guy de Beauchamp, then resident of the manor house. About 100 years later, the house was let to Sir Ralph Bracebridge who, to cultivate fish, built the dam of the pool now bearing his name. Likewise, in the reign of Henry VI, John Holte, keeper of the Chase, constructed Keeper's Pool for the Lenten fish.

The lords of Sutton ended the Wars of the Roses on the losing side and the lands of the Chase were forfeited to the King. Subsequently Henry VIII gave the tract of land to Bishop Vesey who, in turn, presented it to the town for ever.

There were several losses by encroachment and the Enclosure Acts also put pressure on the Park. There was one proposal,

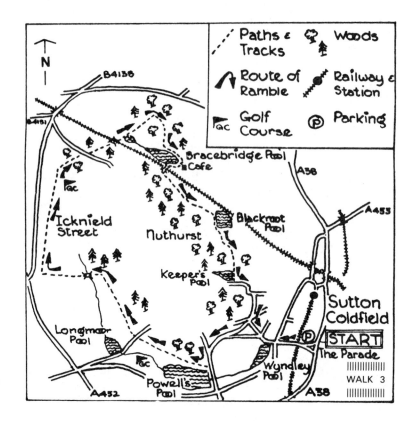

Paths & Tracks · **Woods** · **Route of Ramble** · **Railway & Station** · **Golf Course** · **Parking**

N

B4138
B4181
Bracebridge Pool
Cafe
A38
A453
Icknield Street
Nuthurst
Blackroot Pool
Keeper's Pool
Longmoor Pool
Sutton Coldfield
START
The Parade
Wyndley Pool
Powell's Pool
A452
A38
WALK 3

fortunately defeated, for the enclosure of the Chase and division of the land among the landlords of the neighbourhood. However, the saddest desecration was in 1871. The Midland Railway wanted to connect their line with the South Staffordshire coalfield, the track bisecting the Park. Despite much opposition, the bill passed through the House of Commons on the promise of cheap coal and the scar on the face of the Chase was allowed on payment of £6,500 for two miles of land.

From the Parade, just off which is a convenient car park, in the centre of Sutton, go up Manor Hill, past a no-through-road sign and along Wyndley Lane. Cross over a main road to the Park (Map 139/114958) and walk alongside Wyndley Pool. Go over the tiny bridge by the ford, then left along the Park road to Powell's Pool. By the waterside, turn right and gradually veer away from the Pool proceeding through holly bushes by the golf course.

14

Climb a sandy slope and the path then goes through the bracken to a road.

Cross straight over the road and keep well to the left of a small fir and birch copse. The way continues over heathland as bleak as a Highland fell. On reaching the lofty hill of Rowton (093968), turn left, down the incline and along a wide track. Go over a sparkling brook and past a clump of fir trees. Just before the boundary of the Park, proceed right along Icknield Street where you will notice that oak trees have been planted alongside the Roman highway.

When another track is met, by a tiny stream, proceed right, then go past a golf green to a lane. Turn right, but leave the road after a few yards by walking left to a bridge under the railway. This brings one to a peaceful mere. Walk across a little bridge and into a silver birch wood, immediately bearing right. At a junction of tracks, turn right to the secluded Bracebridge Pool. A charming path winds through the trees to a boathouse and café (101979), a good place to watch the wildfowl.

Leaving the Pool, proceed over the rail bridge. Turn left at once and walk through leaf-carpeted woodland. On meeting a track, bear left through a wooden gate then leave the main path by veering right, through another gate. Cross over a path to reach the placid Blackroot Pool. Do not walk over the dam but proceed straight ahead — to Keeper's Pool. Go along the causeway, then turn left along a narrow road.

Continue past a car park and, after about 200 yards, proceed to the right, by a fire notice. Pass through a large gate (not the nearby kissing gate), and follow a macadamed track. Cross a road and go immediately left, through a gate down to Wyndley Pool and so back to Sutton.

Doubtless, covetous eyes are continuously focused on the beautiful Park and there are those who have ideas that the land should be 'developed' for commercial or leisure purposes. The words of a guide published in 1869, however, are still very relevant: 'Long may the trustees of this unique nook of natural beauty take the same liberal view of their moral obligation in respect to its acres of wild scenery — not to regard them as a means of mere personal enjoyment, not to value them simply as a source of income, an adjunct to a charity estate; but remembering by whom and when they were granted, to look on them as a Royal trust and therefore a popular right, the legacy of ancient times to the toiling millions of our haunts of industry, to be handed down unimpaired to our posterity.'

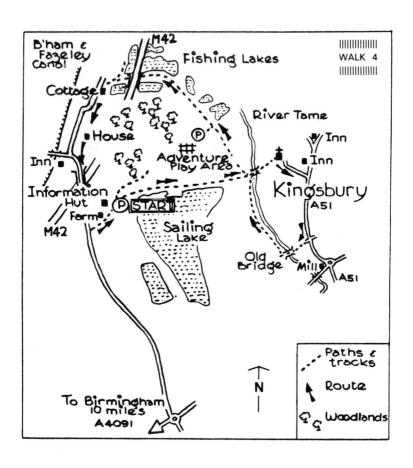

KINGSBURY WATER PARK

WALK 4

★

3½ miles (5.5 km)

OS Landranger 139

Until recently, the name Kingsbury was synonymous with the despoliation caused by the extensive working of sand and gravel in the flat valley of the river Tame. Now many folk actually visit the area since, after much thoughtful planning and skilful work by the Warwickshire County Council, Kingsbury Water Park has been established.

What I especially like about the scheme is that there are so many varied interests that can be accommodated on what was once such inhospitable terrain. Already there are sailing and hydroplane clubs which use the large lake on different days while the angler can obtain day tickets at a modest price to try and outwit the bream, carp, tench, roach, perch and pike.

For children, an exciting adventure playground is situated discreetly near one of the car parks. How I wished on my visit that I was a year or two younger so that I could clamber over these weird and wonderful constructions!

For the naturalist, there is a whole world of interest and fascination. Flowers of the marsh and waterside abound and many birds use the parkland as a resting place on their passages of migration.

There are many pathways over the six hundred acres of the water park which have been left in a semi-wild state and some of these, together with a visit to the village of Kingsbury, provide a pleasant ramble. Entrance to the Park is free but a charge is made for car parking.

There are car parks in the Park. From the one on the Bodymoor Heath Lane (off the A4097) — the map reference is 204960 — take the path going directly away from the road. Within a few steps walk alongside the large lake called Bodymoor Heath Water (used for sailing).

On the other side of the fine pathway is a grassed area where ballgames can be played and kites flown. (This grassed area was once another pool but it was filled with pulverised waste from power stations.) Out of the bushes the path is now on a raised platform since this was an area which was subject to flooding from the river.

We cross the river. The water, during past ages, has eroded the sandstone, leaving the village of Kingsbury high above the cliffs. The ridge is dominated by two buildings; to the left is Kingsbury Hall and alongside, the sturdy tower and church of SS Peter and Paul.

The Hall was once a castle or, perhaps, a fortified house. Parts of the curtain wall remain, together with a tower and an archway but the present house is from the late medieval period. Some authorities suggest that the castle may have been occupied by the King of Mercia.

In the church we can see much of the work of the Normans although there was said to have been considerable rebuilding around the early 14th century when the tower was constructed.

There are a couple of inns in Kingsbury but the ramble continues by walking a short distance to the right along the A51. Just before you proceed off the main road, you can see the tall structure of Kingsbury Mill. This has been a mill-site since ancient times — it was listed at the Domesday survey.

Cross the three arches of an old bridge which has been 'pensioned-off' as regards carrying motor traffic. Over the river Tame, go into the waterside meadows to the right where the pathway follows the side of the river to our earlier crossing place.

Stay to the left of a playing field to reach a track going off to the left. (This leads to another car park and the adventure play area.) The route of the ramble, however, is not to the left but straight on alongside lakes which are landscaped to provide facilities for canoeists and for children to sail boats.

When I walked these paths, a chorus of waterbirds heralded the arrival overhead of a huge flock of about eighty greylag geese which were making a courtesy call from the lakes of Packington Park.

We now have lakes on both sides. These are bordered by willows which hang low and there is more beauty in the 'cups and saucers' of the white and yellow water-lilies. The path leads under a motorway, then goes sharp left at a former brick and timber farmstead, and along a lane. At a road proceed to the left, to the entrance to the Water Park. Here there is an information centre which explains the natural features of the geology and wildlife of a rejuvenated region that now provides much fun and enjoyment.

SHUSTOKE, NETHER WHITACRE AND FOUL END

WALK 5

★

8 miles (13 km)

OS Landranger 139 and 140

When I was mapping out a ramble around Shustoke I noted a place called Foul End.

Surely a title such as this could not be as bad as it sounded, I thought; I wondered why, like other strange names, slight alterations over the centuries could not have resulted in something more pleasant. Perhaps it once belonged to Squire Fowler.

The locals I asked could not give an answer to the derivation of the name and, in any case, it was rather a misnomer; in spite of the proximity of coal mines, we find an area intensively farmed. Other places nearby are more indicative of an attractive landscape — Rushy Flanders, Gnomon Wood and Nether Whitacre.

Shustoke was the home of that great antiquarian and historian of the Midland counties, Sir William Dugdale. In the 17th century he chronicled much fascinating material of our churches, buildings and life of that time.

During the Civil War he lived dangerously and his travels took him to the battle at Edgehill but happily, he survived to die at his home, Blythe Hall, a mile or so from Shustoke.

It is interesting to read that Dugdale married when he was only seventeen and his bride was a year younger. There is a monument to Sir William in the hilltop church of St Cuthbert. This building dates from Norman times although there was much rebuilding in the 19th century after a fire started by lightning.

There are quiet roads south of the B4114 in Shustoke suitable for parking. From the centre of the village, walk past the inn and post office with its neat garden and along the B4114 towards Coleshill (Map 139/226909). Just beyond a lane to the left, is a kissing gate on the opposite side of the road, adjoining a vehicle track.

There is now a well-used pathway across a pasture.

Over a brook, the path crosses a field. Do not go over the

19

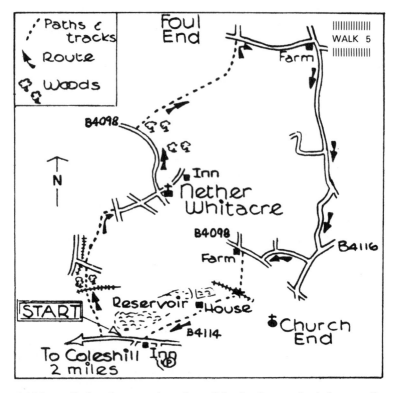

hidden stile but keep at the edge of the hedge on the left to a stile which gives access to a railway.

After a 'Stop, Look and Listen' sign, proceed over the tracks to another stile and a footpath through a copse. We now border another field which is sometimes under cultivation to reach a lane (221918). Turn left for a few yards to a path which starts next to the railway. A pleasant way now — unspectacular but gentle paths.

The clear track bears away from the railway. Just past a 'Warning' notice go through a hedge gap on the right and continue so the hedge is now on your left to a fence stile. Keep the hedge on the left and go over a stile to a large arable field.

Aim for the left-hand black and white house. There is no definite stile to cross the far boundary. Now in a pasture, continue with the hedge on your right side to a stile in the far corner. Turn 90 degrees right and walk to a lane (225927). To the right and left are some 'olde-worlde' cottages which have seen many summers — and will, without doubt, witness many more. Almost opposite our way is Deep Lane to Nether Whitacre.

20

Deep Lane crosses two roads and becomes Dog Lane with the Dog Inn just beyond the church. The church has the appearance of a building of great age but, in fact, only the tower dates back beyond the last century.

Retrace your steps to the last crossroads and walk right about half a mile along the B4098. Beyond woodland, proceed to the right along a no-through-road (226936). The shady lane soon becomes a bridleway and crosses a stream.

Keep straight ahead to reach a large field. Turn 90 degrees left (wire on the left) to a deep ditch and follow this to the right. The bridleway leads to a field gate and a farm track which has a hedge each side.

The farm way climbs to the ridge of Foul End where, on a lane, continue right by New House Farm. At a T-junction, turn right — the route being signed to Over Whitacre.

When the lane divides, our way is to the right. The little road climbs steadily and may be flanked by tall grasses — uncut and therefore supporting a myriad of insect life and allowing plants to seed. Keep ahead at the next junction (Nether Whitacre).

At the B4116, walk to the right, then right again along Pound Lane to the B4098. A short distance along the main road to the right we come to an unsigned footpath.

Go through a little ornate metal gate by the main gate of Old Farm. Cross to a gate to a meadow. Aim for the stile in the bottom right-hand corner. Climb further stiles then veer left to a metal footbridge over a brook. Sharp right is a tunnel under the railway.

Stay on the path to the right, keeping to the left of a wood.

The route is indicated by a series of stiles and borders Shustoke Reservoir. We join the vehicle track which leads back to Shustoke.

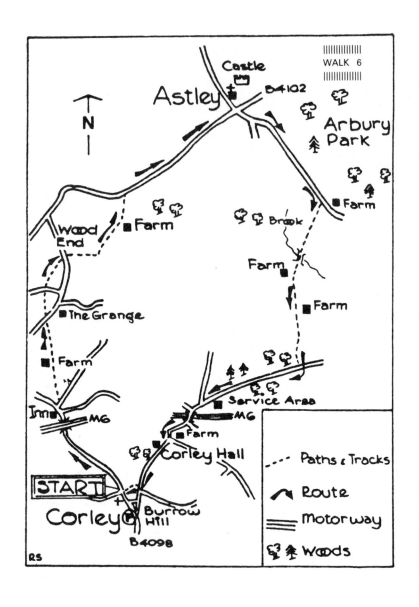

CORLEY AND ASTLEY

WALK 6

★

8 miles (13 km)

OS Landranger 140

'The village lay in the central plain of what we are pleased to call Merry England and held farms which, speaking from a spiritual point of view, paid highly desirable tithes.'

This description comes from George Eliot's *Silas Marner*, written more than 100 years ago. George Eliot was born on the estate of Arbury, near Nuneaton, where her father was an agent. She was said to have been a keen walker in her childhood and her vivid word pictures of the countryside were no doubt influenced by her rambles in that corner of North-East Warwickshire.

George Eliot now seems rather unfashionable. In these days when visiting places of literary interest is popular, it is perhaps unfortunate that she lived in a somewhat inauspicious area. If only her home had been in a town nestling at the edge of the Cotswolds!

Her novel *Felix Holt* has fine descriptions of the landscape in its opening pages and Corley Hall, which we pass on this walk, is a Jacobean house said to have been the Hall Farm in *Adam Bede*. This is disputed by some researchers but surely some literary licence is allowable to popularise a great weaver of tales of the Midland counties.

So let us venture deep into the countryside of 'dewy brambles and rank, tufted grass'.

The starting place is Corley, on the B4098, north west of Coventry, a hamlet perched on a bracing ridge, about 600 feet above sea level. There is a lay-by, where one can park, just south of Corley church. An extensive Iron Age fort enclosing seven acres was built on the slopes of nearby Burrow Hill and the earthworks are still conspicuous. The church of Corley dates from Norman times and has a font inscribed 1661.

From the church (Map 140/302852), walk along the B4098 towards Tamworth. Go under a motorway bridge. Opposite an inn, turn right along Square Lane (caution — there are two roads) and after a few yards, turn left along a path through a metal gate. Cross a field to a fence opposite, then pass a small pond and keep to the right of old farm buildings and a garden to a stile.

Cut across a meadow to a stile leading to sheepwalks. Gradually leave the left-hand hedge and walk to a stile on a lane (292869). Cross to the stile almost opposite then climb another. The path continues by a left-hand hedge. In the next field, keep a hedge (where there is evidence of rabbit burrows) on the left to a quiet lane.

Walk straight across the lane to a stile (which lies well back off the road just to the left of a white cottage) leading into a field. Continue through a wooden gate, then go alongside a hedge on the left. Proceed to a stile into an adjacent field, where there is a pond. Now walk on the original heading, with the fence on the right and at the road (294878), climb a stile almost opposite. This gives access to a pasture and the path bears round to the right, alongside the hedge.

There is soon a sharp kink in the hedge. Look carefully for a stile into a sometimes cultivated field and proceed with the hedge now on the left. Go over a corner fence stile to immediately turn 90 degrees left and walk beside a pool.

Pass under power cables, then aim for a hidden stile situated a few yards to the right of the corner of the field. Continue over a brook and into a field. Veering slightly right, aim towards a wire fence by a huge dead-looking tree. In the meadow beyond, proceed to a metal gate onto a farm drive. Turn left, then right on the B4102 (301883).

This road leads to Astley. The massive tower of the church, dedicated to St Mary, dominates the skyline. This is a fascinating building. Built originally as a collegiate church in 1343, it was cruciform with a central tower and spire.

After the Reformation, the church fell into disrepair and the spire and tower collapsed about 1600. A few years later the huge chancel became the nave of a restored church and a new chancel and tower were added. Behind the church is Astley Castle, once the home of the Greys, the tragic Lady Jane Grey's family.

We continue the walk from the church by crossing over the B4102 and along a lane signposted to Corley. Keep straight ahead at the next junction and over to the left is George Eliot's Arbury estate. (The hall was built on the site of an Augustinian priory and is sometimes open to the public.)

Follow the little lane for about a mile. Just before a farm on the brow of a hill, turn right through a metal gate. A clear track can be seen going across the open, pastoral countryside. Go over the wide stream and, as the track sweeps right to the farm, veer slightly left through a metal gate to soon reach a road (320865).

Turn right to the complex of motorway buildings and concrete — a noisy and permanent intrusion into the rural scene. Go over

24

the highway and past a farm, then right along Rock Lane. Walk past Corley Hall where there is an ancient gateway in the middle of the front garden, the pillars topped by heraldic griffins. 'That gate is never opened,' wrote George Eliot.

By the white-gated Rock House, go through a kissing gate. Climb the pasture to a stile in the top right-hand corner. In the next field, follow the left-hand hedge to a white cottage opposite Corley church to complete the pastoral ramble in the lands of George Eliot.

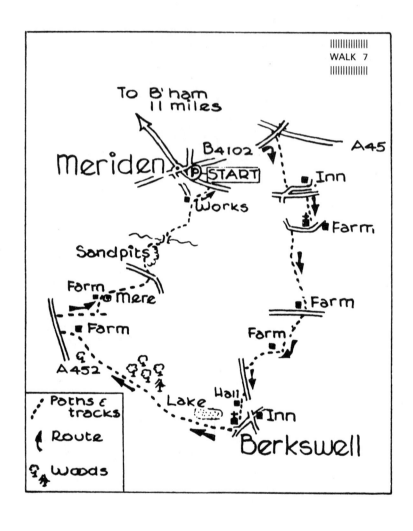

THE CENTRE OF ENGLAND

★

8 miles (13 km)

OS Landranger 139 and 140

By tradition, the trim village green of Meriden marks the centre of England. I do not know how the place was singled out for this distinction or how the distances are measurable with our indented coastline. Perhaps the lines to the centre were bent a little to Meriden because there was a large village green — convenient for meetings and gatherings over the ages.

'Meriden' is an attractive name but actually it means something like 'miry vale'. However, although low-lying, the village has a reputation for being healthy and it escaped when the Great Plague was rife in 1665. It is a convenient and pleasant spot to begin a ramble.

Park alongside the green at Meriden. Then, from the ancient wayside cross, which has stood on the village site for 500 years, go along the Fillongley Road (B4102). After three-quarters of a mile, just before the road bridge over a main highway, turn right along a signposted field path (Map reference 248827).

Go over a stile into a field (which may be cultivated) and continue beside the left-hand hedge. Over another stile, the hedge soon goes 90 degrees left. The path, however, continues on the same heading as before across the field to the stile opposite. Walk around the edge of the next field, then aim to the left of a row of bungalows. On the road turn left.

Climb steps opposite the Queen's Head inn; go through a metal gate (252820) on the far side of the main road. A fine path leads us through woodland and fields then along the edge of the churchyard of the ancient church of St Lawrence. The building dates from Norman times but a notice states rather cryptically that 'the original foundation was by Lady Godiva'.

On the left is the timber and brick Moat House Farm which bears a date 1609. On the lane, proceed right and go past the church gate. As the road bends sharply, a signed path starts on the left. Proceed to the far left-hand corner of the field and walk through a gap in the hedge to a farm track.

Continue on the same heading, with a hedge on the left,

27

through a beautiful pastoral landscape. Over a new stile (by the site marked on the 1:25,000 map as St Lawrence's Well) keep on the same bearing. Through a metal gate, bear left across the pasture to a wooden gate, by an oak tree. Continue to a metal gate and, in the next meadow, go up the incline towards a farmhouse.

There is now a double stile. Aim to the left of old barns to a farm drive leading to a lane (254805). Cross straight over to a stile. In the field walk with a hedge on the left. Soon bear right and proceed through a meadow and a sometimes sown field, now with a hedge on the right. Waymarks show the way.

By a stagnant pond, go over a stile and walk to the left of another pool, then across the pasture to a metal gate. Turn right to a farm drive (Blind Lane). At a road, go to the left. After 200 yards, proceed through a kissing gate on the right. There is now a delightful path bordering the parkland of Berkswell Hall.

We arrive at the picture-book village of Berkswell by, according to an authority on buildings, 'the most interesting Norman church in Warwickshire'. But there are other things in this fascinating place. For instance, the well-preserved stocks with five holes; the odd number being explained by the legend that one place was reserved for an old gentleman with a wooden leg. Nearby is a huge well, restored, so a notice tells us, by public subscription in 1851; it is thought to have been used for immersion baptisms by the monks of Lichfield.

The walk is resumed by going past a unique 16th century porch to the church. With a gable that would look right on a country cottage, the porch has some beautiful timberwork. Beyond the churchyard, the path borders a stream and goes through woodland to a metal kissing gate. Cross the park road opposite (240790) where there is a path signposted to Hampton.

Out of the parkland, the way goes around the edge of several fields, then into a pine wood. Leave the trees by climbing a stile into a meadow. Stay on the same heading with a hedge on the left. Walk to a farm drive which leads to the A452.

Proceed to the right but only stay on the main highway for about a quarter of a mile, then turn right along a signposted bridleway. When the farm road divides, take the left-hand fork and go past the old Merecot Mill, the decaying mill wheel of which can be seen inside the building.

Turn right and go by a wood. In a meadow, walk parallel to the right-hand fence. The path is arrowed to a road (235809). Turn right a few steps, on the opposite side of the road is a double stile. Take care here as diversions are frequent. The pathway goes above sandpits and on a hot summer's day one might fancy one was on a Sahara ramble! Out of the 'desert', walk to the 'oasis' where there is a plank bridge over a stream. The way, fenced by wire, now 'dog-legs' to the right then left up an incline. Near the top of the ridge, opposite a bank of sand, go through a field gate on the right. In the meadow walk in a diagonal direction. Cross a ditch over a plank bridge. Keeping on much the same diagonal heading, we go over the pastures back to the centre of England.

KENILWORTH CASTLE

WALK 8

★

6½ miles or 3½ miles (10.5 or 5.5 km)

OS Landranger 139 and 140

There can be few more stirring places to begin a ramble in the counties of the Midlands than Kenilworth where so much of our history was enacted. A great authority on the buildings of England was moved to call Kenilworth Castle one of the grandest ruined castles with 'superb' Norman, 14th century and Elizabethan work. This is the place where one can read an outline of history, the battles and intrigue, the feastings and celebrations — and then allow the imagination to have a field-day.

There were several great periods of building but it would seem to have been Geoffrey de Clinton who started the grandiose scheme in 1125. He was from a humble family but rose to be Henry I's Chief Justice and Treasurer and decided that the rock near the brook would make an ideal and worthy site for his home.

The next Henry favoured the place himself and added the keep about fifty years after Clinton's early beginnings. King John's contribution was great, with an expenditure of £2,000. Next, as with many other buildings of the day, John of Gaunt, the Duke of Lancaster, set about improving the castle, and his additions turned the place away from being a harsh, fortress-like structure.

Robert Dudley is said to have spent £60,000 on the famous seventeen-day visit by Queen Elizabeth. Every ingenious device was used to create spectacle; there was music from the minstrels, fireworks and pageants and much feasting. But less than 100 years later the days of splendour of the castle were over and it became a ruin when the Parliamentarians tore down its walls and defences.

Park in the car park by Kenilworth Castle and start the ramble from Castle Green. There are many attractive cottages here and, across the road, are finely restored houses at Little Virginia where the potato is said to have been planted after being introduced from foreign parts.

Walk along the vehicle way called Purlieu Lane and cross a brook. (Two streams, Finham and Inchford Brooks, were used in

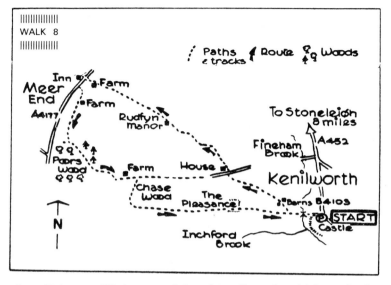

far off days to fill the great lake of Kenilworth, which made the castle so impenetrable.) Immediately over Finham Brook, take a path on the right (Map 140/276724).

Proceed diagonally over a pasture along a waymarked path. Go through a metal gate by barns and again our way crosses fields, towards a small copse. Beyond, climb a fence and continue to a lane by a red-brick house. Turn left on the lane for the shorter route.

However, if you wish to take the longer route, cross to another field path signposted to Meer End and keep following the yellow arrows. Go over a pasture to a stile. There is then another stile giving access to fields often sown. Stay on the same heading to cross a bridge and continue to a crossing hedge. There is then a sharp turn to the left to keep a hedge on the right and take us by a pool. Follow the edge of the field around to the right to a field gate. Do not proceed to Chase Farm but, through the gate, go to the left under electricity cables.

Leave the field border and head right towards an old farmstead. Walk by a barn and over the drive in front of Rudfyn Manor, a lovely black timber and brick house. The route, still waymarked over several stiles, proceeds at the side of a field to a stile near a brick bungalow. Through a gateway, bear left to a gate across a pasture and by the farmhouse we join the drive to the A4177 and an inn (246744).

The inn used to have a piece of music on the sign. For the non-musical rambler the notice on the inn explained 'In

31

remembrance of Harry Williams of Tipperary Fame . . . world famous song which helped to save Old England.' Harry Williams, who wrote the song with Jack Judge, lived here when the place was called The Plough.

The ramble resumes a few yards away from the inn, opposite a white cottage. Go over a stile and along a footpath — still look out for the marking arrows. After 100 yards turn right. Keep on this constant general direction, over stiles and bordering pastureland and beyond a metal kissing gate walk through a meadow to a stile by Poors Wood. Turn left — blue arrows now.

Past Blackhill Wood on the left — a plantation of Scots fir, which adds a delicate fragrance to the cooling breeze — and the wide track swings around to the right. Through a gateway, go sharp left and follow the vehicle track by farm buildings.

Beyond, continue along a footpath which is signed to Honiley to the right (253728). Away on the far ridge we can see the village church, said to have been influenced by Sir Christopher Wren who lived nearby at Wroxall Abbey.

Keep on the sandy track beside Chase Wood, then turn left at the bottom of the slope. We soon see again the marvellous castle and you will agree that this really is the most impressive approach to it.

Before rejoining the outward route, we go over ridges and ditches in a meadow. These are not the earthworks of some ancient fortification but the site of the Pleasance, a summer house built about 1414 by Henry V for the kings of the 15th century found the timber-framed building more comfortable than the grand state apartments of the castle. Henry VIII did another demolition job here.

One further thought at the end of this ramble. All the pathways on this walk have been waymarked by public-spirited footpath societies. Not only do these marks eliminate much of the frustration of a rambler who might have doubts about the correct right of way but they also diminish the risk of damage and reduce a source of friction between rambler and landowner.

HARBURY AND CHESTERTON MILL

WALK 9

★

6½ miles (10.5 km)

OS Landranger 151

There are many 'lost' villages in the Midland counties where nothing remains of them except perhaps a field name or the furrows and hollows of earthworks. Chesterton has little except a gem of a meticulously maintained church at the end of a lane to nowhere. The heart of Chesterton was lost almost two hundred years ago when the great mansion of the Peyto family was destroyed by John Peyto in 1802.

There are plenty of reminders of the Peytos, however. The church has some massive monuments, tombs and effigies and outside is a pedimented gateway which was the family's private entrance from the house across the meadows. The bricks and tiles of the gateway have weathered since Inigo Jones built it in 1632.

Inigo Jones is also credited with the windmill on the nearby hilltop. This beautiful design of curves and arches was rescued from its derelict state during a Civic Trust Architectural Heritage Year competition and won a highly acclaimed award.

Harbury is the starting place for this walk. Here, there is another windmill. The village was in the news in the 1920s when the skeleton of a prehistoric monster was found in quarries nearby; the bones now reside in the Natural History Museum in London.

Park in one of Harbury's quiet streets, then, from the centre of the village, walk along Park Lane, past the Old New Inn (still pretty ancient and pretty, too, with tall hollyhocks against the walls). Look for a stile on the opposite side of the road (Map 151/367597). In a meadow, keep by the fence then cross several other fields and border the line of a stream and willow trees to a lane. Turn right, then take the left-hand fork at a junction.

At the next meeting of roads is the start of the green footpath to Chesterton Mill. The mill has been here since 1632 — but was it built as a working mill or as a glorious folly to satisfy the aesthetic taste of the Peytos?

Having pondered this problem, return to the lane and road

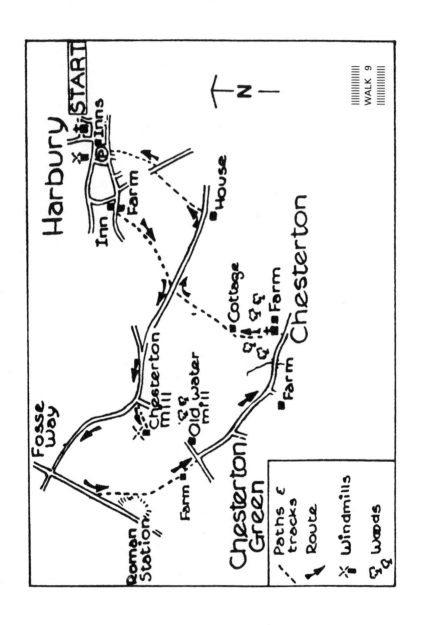

WALK 9

34

junction and proceed to the left to the road of the Romans, Fosse Way (344603).

This road can be quite busy so we soon leave it by going along in the direction indicated by a bridleway sign on the left. The track (undefined) skirts the squared outline of the Roman station (which, I understand, has not been excavated to date). Join a farm track and go to the left of farm buildings to a road (345589).

Cross to a lane — a rustic way which goes to Chesterton Green and over a stream to Chesterton church. St Giles' Church has a long battlement parapet, a Norman font and ancient sculptures from around the year 1400. Whoever composed the motto over the porch doorway — 'See and be gone about your business' — did not realise that one may wish to linger awhile in this peaceful spot.

Before you leave, check the hour by the ancient sundial. The next path starts at the back of the churchyard. Near the farm cottage is a gate giving access to the pasture. Go down the slope to a bridge over a stream in the trees.

In the next field, cross diagonally to a stile at the left of an old cottage which, I was informed, was once part of the stables of the Peyto mansion which was near this place. The only other reminder here is the tall brick wall that once protected the crops of the kitchen garden.

Over the stile, keep by the hedge of a large field to a lane. We were here on the outward journey but the walk now continues to the right, for about half a mile. Opposite a gated and arched entrance to a house, climb a stile on the left and walk to a lane where another stile and footpath are to be found a couple of yards to the right. This way leads back by a sports field to Harbury.

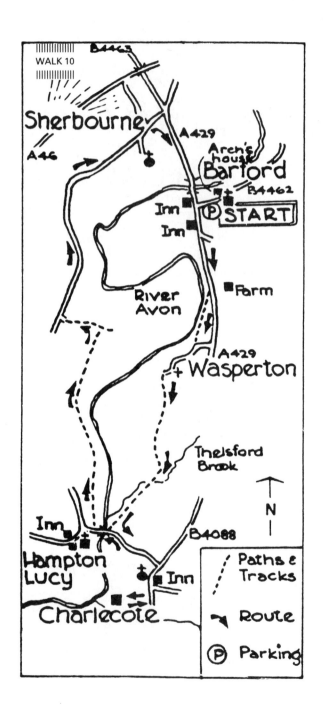

CHARLECOTE AND HAMPTON LUCY

WALK 10

7 miles (11 km)

OS Landranger 151

This walk features a contrast of living styles. At the beginning of the ramble is the little village of Barford, three or four miles to the south of Warwick. Here lived Joseph Arch, the pioneer campaigner for the welfare of the agricultural labourer who, even as an MP, continued to live in the tiny cottage by the church. One of the inns in the village is named after him.

Further down the Avon vale is the huge mansion of Charlecote Park, home of the Lucy family and now owned by the National Trust. The place has been part of the tourist's Shakespeare circuit for 200 years or so and who would dare dispute the connection, although the links are rather tenuous?

Legend has it that the then-young William was caught poaching deer by the owner, Sir Thomas Lucy, and Mr Justice Shallow in *The Merry Wives of Windsor* who has a coat containing a 'dozen white luces' (freshwater fishes) is reputed to be a mocking portrait of the noble Sir Thomas.

This ramble cannot conveniently be shortened as there are few bridges over the river Avon.

Park along the B4462 in Barford. The walk starts with something of a challenge at some seasons. From the centre of Barford, go along the Stow Road for three-quarters of a mile. Just past Forge Cottage and opposite the drive to Holloway Farm, turn right (Map 151/271597). Here comes the challenge as the riverside path can be bordered by nettles. Just before a holiday hut, climb the bank on the left to enter a field. Stay by the hedge to a lane (some walkers omit the riverside path and follow the line of the hedge from the A429).

Turn right to the hamlet of Wasperton. The little church of St John the Baptist was renovated early in the career of Sir Gilbert Scott and has an open wooden bell turret. The lane soon becomes a rough bridleway, going to the left. Walk through several gates, then by farmland. At a signed junction of paths turn right along a bridleway.

Go left through a hunting gate to cross Thelsford Brook. At

37

once go right through another hunting gate. Walk to the far end of a meadow. Walk not far from the stream. Climb over waymarked stiles to eventually arrive at a road by Charlecote Mill. Turn left. A leafy way goes alongside the parkland of Charlecote and is a good place from which to admire the beautiful deer.

A right turn on the B4088 brings us to the mansion. Allow a good measure of time to visit the house, built in the shape of the letter 'E' (which is said to have flattered Queen Elizabeth I), to see its lovely orangery, and also to linger in the gardens, laid out by Capability Brown.

Retrace your steps along the B4088 and continue to the left to Hampton Lucy. Here is the church of St Peter, which must surely be the finest modern church of the country — if one can call a building 150 years old modern! Designed at the time of the Gothic revival by Thomas Rickman it was commissioned by the Rev John Lucy of Charlecote.

Continuing the ramble, walk along a bridleway going north by the bridge over the Avon (257572). Immediately leave the main track. The route has now been waymarked with arrows for some distance but caution is required early on when the path climbs a pasture on the left. This is a fine lofty way with extensive vistas of the lush meadows of the meandering river. Take care by a wood as the path goes slightly left into a field and alongside the hedge, not along the better defined track through the trees.

More field paths bring us near the summit of the quaintly named Copdock Hill. Walk through a nearby gate, then resume the original heading. The path is now over an open field by the row of trees marking the former hedge line. At the far hedge turn right for 100 yards then go through a hedge gap to a bordering field. Resume the old heading to a lane. Proceed left (258594). If you glance back from this high viewpoint you realise that, even today, Arden is an extensive area of 'greenwood trees'.

At the junction of a lane, turn right. Two miles along this peaceful way is the little village of Sherbourne. A trim place this; the churchyard has held the trophy for being the best-maintained in the Diocese of Coventry.

A right turn on the A429 returns the rambler to Barford to complete the walk along the valley of the Avon.

BADDESLEY CLINTON AND WROXALL ABBEY

WALK 11

8 miles (13 km)

OS Landranger 139

It was Shakespeare who summarised the therapeutic benefits derived from a country ramble when he wrote:
>Jog on, jog on the footpath way,
>And merrily hent the stile-a;
>A merry heart goes all the day,
>Your sad tires in a mile-a.

On this walk, we jog along lovely paths to visit some fine old buildings—a moated Tudor manor house, an abbey on the site of a priory and a Norman church.

The walk begins from the Roman Catholic church of St Francis, along a lane at Baddesley Clinton, just off the A41 road (Map 139/208724). Here there is a convenient lay-by for parking. We pass the Poor Clares' Convent — the order was founded by St Francis of Assisi in 1212 and the convent was established in 1850 by nuns from Bruges.

At a road junction, take the left-hand fork and go past Park Farm. By the ornate pillars at the drive to a recently-converted house, Brome Park, walk along a field path on the right. We soon veer left to keep to the edge of Badgers Coppice (on the right-hand side) and remain on this heading to meet the drive of Baddesley Clinton Hall.

This medieval manor house is surrounded by water and has been the seat of the Ferrers family since 1517. During the days of Roman Catholic persecution, many priests are said to have found refuge in the hides of the mansion. The edifice contains a mixture of building styles with much Elizabethan work while the bridge over the moat is about 200 years old and is especially beautiful.

The footpaths on the estate are well signposted and our way is straight over the drive, through a hunting gate and over the meadows. From here, there is a good view of the house and the stables, which date from the 17th century, beyond.

Over a stile, go over further stiles and a brook. Keep in this direction until you reach a pasture which has a good crop of huge

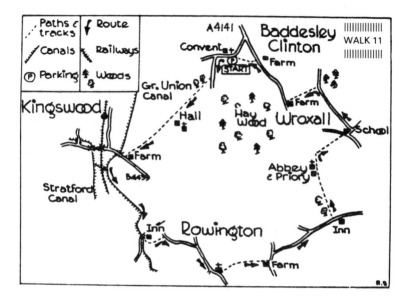

electricity pylons. The path now cuts diagonally across the field to the far right-hand corner, where there is a stile and a farm track leading to the B4439 (192708).

Turn right for a short distance to the towing path of the Grand Union Canal. This waterway was built as the Warwick and Birmingham Canal and was opened in 1793. Walking along the towpath to the left, we come to Kingswood Junction, where the Stratford-upon-Avon Canal is connected. This was, in its heyday, a lucrative place as the Warwick and Birmingham Company exacted the price of a lock of water for every boat which passed over the junction.

By Bridge 63 at Turner's Green, where there are some quaint waterside cottages and an inn, you will see a footpath sign on the road to the right of the inn. Follow the direction indicated. Keep to the edge of a field to a vehicle track, then to a lane, where turn right, then right again on the B4439.

We are now in the village of Rowington. The church of St Lawrence has stood on its hilltop site since Norman times — the original north wall remains but the building was widened in the late 13th century to its present width. The figures on the old sundial are barely visible but the church clock tells us to be on the move again.

A field path starts at the far end of the churchyard, alongside the road. Climb a stile into a meadow and descend the slope to further stiles. Cut across to a metal gate situated on a bridge over a brook. The path now goes straight across the field and up the hill, keeping well to the left of a field depression containing trees, to a gap in the hedge.

Continue up the incline (hedge on left). At the top of the ridge, keep the hedge and old farm on your right. Walk beside (not along) the farm drive to a lane (213694). Turn left, then right at a road junction, and follow quiet lanes for about a mile. Just before an inn with the unusual name 'Case is Altered', take a footpath to the left (rough stile). Across a pasture and over a stile, walk to the right of an elongated copse and gradually leave the edge of the field to reach a kissing gate adjacent to the wood ahead.

The massive building of Wroxall Abbey can now be seen. Nearby is the site of the priory founded by Benedictine nuns about 1135; little now remains except part of the church and cloisters. The large house now called Wroxall Abbey was built, in typical heavy Victorian style, towards the end of the last century and replaced an earlier Elizabethan structure. Sir Christopher Wren bought the estate three years after his St Paul's Cathedral was completed in 1713, when he was over 80.

Cross the drive and go alongside a wall and a pool. Walk through a metal gate and then to a splendid avenue of oak trees to arrive at another drive. Proceed right, through sheep pastures to the A4141. By a school to the right, leave the main road along a lane, but immediately take the way on the left.

Now look for a metal gate on the left; ensure you are at the right place — there should be a large wood almost opposite. Turn left through the gate, into pasture land. A bridleway now follows the line of the hedge to emerge on the A4141 again, by Abbey Farm.

Proceed to the right and keep on the road for about half a mile. Almost opposite a farm drive, turn left along a wide track. The way is soon barred by a field gate, so walk to the right, into a meadow. This field path goes back to Baddesley Clinton.

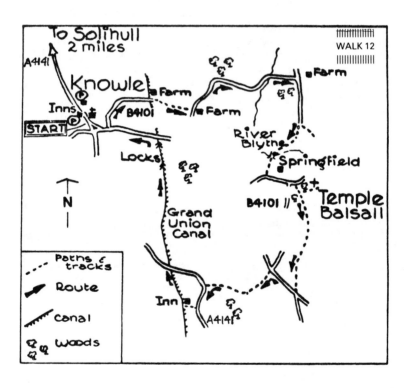

KNOWLE AND TEMPLE BALSALL

WALK 12

★

5 miles (8 km)

OS Landranger 139

This short ramble takes us through the Warwickshire countryside to the home of the Knights Templars at Temple Balsall. The Knights Templars were instituted in 1118 and received this name as they first lived in rooms adjoining the Temple in Jerusalem. The worthy brethren guarded the road taken by the pilgrims to the Holy Land and came to England at the time of King Stephen. The lands in the parish of Hampton-in-Arden were given to the order by Roger de Mowbray. The Knights Templars built their house and chapel; the chapel, although much restored, remains to this day and is now the parish church of St Mary.

I started the walk from Knowle. Here there are more fine old buildings but the real gems are the guild house and the church. The place of worship has dedications to St John the Baptist, St Lawrence and St Anne and was built during the reign of Richard II when there were hardly fifty houses in the village. The guild house, the work of Walter Cook, served as a popular place of learning for the local nobility.

Leave the car in one of the car parks off the High Street in Knowle and, from the timbered guild house next to the church, go a short distance along the B4101 towards Warwick. Turn left along Kixley Lane (Map 139/184766).

Over the Grand Union Canal there is a signposted field path. Cross a little brook. Veer right to a hedge and follow the edge of a pasture to Elvers Green Farm and a lane. Turn left.

The lane twists and turns and then a ford is reached but there is a footbridge over the river Blythe. At a T-junction, by the elaborate gateway of Barston Park Farm, our way is right along a track marked as a no-through-road for motors. The tarmac ends at a house which is proud to announce that it dates from the days of Queen Anne.

Follow a direction over a stile and across an open landscape towards the grounds of Springfield House, a brick mansion built in the last century and once the seat of the Boultbee family. It is now a residential school.

The track goes over an old bridge spanning the river Blythe. These lands were formerly the gardens of the mansion, and I disturbed a large flock of lapwings beside the water. By a children's playground, where there are some marvellous things over which youngsters can scramble, bear right and go to the rear of the buildings. The pathway is clearly signed to the B4101 (201761).

Proceed to the left to a road junction where you will see a footpath going into a copse on the right. This lovely path leads to Temple Balsall. Beyond the church are the cottages for senior citizens — the oldest buildings have been here for three hundred years. They were endowed by Katherine Leveson, granddaughter of Robert Dudley who was a great favourite of Queen Elizabeth I.

South of the church is the ancient hall, or refectory, of the knights. Retrace your steps to the copse where there is a kissing gate on the left leading into a field. The path leads to a farm track. You should then have a hedge on your left. By keeping to the borders of several fields, a lane is reached (206748).

Go to the right for about a third of a mile, to a junction of roads. On the left, along the drive of a house, a footpath starts. This becomes an attractive way through wooded dells and brings us to a farm track where we continue to the right, through gateways, to the A4141. A few yards to the left is a way to the Black Boy inn and the canal. Proceed along the towpath to the right.

There is now an interesting stretch of the waterway with a succession of locks which take craft up the lofty Knowle ridge. As I walked back to our starting place a flight of geese in V-formation soared across the winter sky and there was a flurry or two of snow in the air. I quickened my step to reach the warmth of my favourite inn at Knowle.

HENLEY AND THE CASTLE
OF THE DE MONTFORTS

WALK 13

★

5 miles (8 km)

OS Landranger 151

The mellowed old town of Henley-in-Arden with its mile-long High Street containing an assortment of fine buildings is not named in the Domesday Book and was no doubt accounted for in the lands of the neighbouring parish of Wootton Wawen.

The first documentary mention of Henley is in a grant of a mill by Henry de Montfort in the reign of Henry II.

However, it is the de Montfort's castle on Beaudesert Mount which we remember today. The motte and bailey fortification was built by Thurstan in the 11th century but when the lord of the manor, Peter, was slain with Simon de Montfort at the battle of Evesham, 1265, the fortune of the once magnificent castle declined.

Now there is little to see except the flattened hilltop and the ditches which mark the lines of the former moat. No doubt many of the ancient buildings of Henley contain timbers and stones from the castle.

There is parking in the High Street in Henley-in-Arden. Walk along the no-through-road of Beaudesert Lane, alongside the 15th century church of St John. Cross the river Alne to the little church of Beaudesert, dedicated to St Nicholas. (It is said there are two churches so close because the river was often flooded and impassable.) The old stones have weathered since the time of the Normans, although the site was once a Saxon place of worship. The building contains fine glasswork and a roof of sturdy Arden oak.

Next to the churchyard, climb the hillock on which stood the castle. The site is impressive, with extensive views over fields which, in Shakespeare's day, were covered with the greenwood trees of the Forest of Arden.

The route descends to the school and a stile onto a hard footpath which leads, to the left, to a road on a new housing estate. Cross the road to another footpath. Here, after a steep climb, there is a good panoramic view of the castle earthworks.

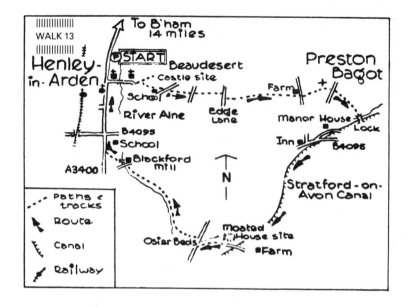

At the top of the hill is a stile to climb. In the field you will see another stile just to the right. Turn to the left after crossing the second stile so that the hedge is on the left-hand side, towards a lane. This is crossed to a gateway, with again the hedgerow to the left, to the old green lane called Edge Lane. An ancient record suggests this may have been a route to the Roman post by Liveridge Hill.

A short distance to the right is a stile which leads to a field. Go straight across, then stay on a fairly constant heading over stiles of various shapes, types and sizes.

When you see a group of buildings at Church Farm the route continues by aiming just to the right so that the lane is reached by a picturesque black and white cottage. There is a signposted footpath opposite which climbs steeply past the former vicarage (larger than the church) to an old seat with the invitation to 'rest and be thankful'.

Nearby is a tall fir tree which I was told was planted by the Reverend Mr Heathfield when he became vicar of Preston Bagot. He retained the incumbency for fifty-five years and preached his last sermon when he was ninety.

The lovely little All Saints' Church, Preston Bagot, is another Norman structure, and inside I met the verger who kindly pointed out the interesting features of the building.

During the reign of Henry II the manor passed to the Earls of

46

Warwick and was sold to Ingeram Bagot, so giving the place the latter part of its name.

Cross over a lane to the start of a field path by a stile and signpost.

The path soon veers to the right to cross a brook and arrive at the Stratford-upon-Avon Canal. This waterway, completed in 1816, bustles with holiday craft in the summer months.

Turn right along the towing path and pass the lock-keeper's cottage with its distinctive barrel-shaped roof which some say was built by Dutchmen.

Beyond a road bridge over the canal, the old building away to the right is the timber-framed manor house, which dates from the 16th century. (A little distance along the road, the Crabmill Inn can be seen.)

The place to leave the canal is well waymarked by arrows on a bridge which carries a farm drive. Walk to the right where, in the meadow alongside, the hollows of the moat to an extensive house are clearly visible. On a lane, we proceed to the right, near to osier beds. In the days before plastics, these provided the basket-maker with his raw material.

The next stile is on the left and, straight across sheep pastures, will be found a pathway which follows the banks of the river Alne up-stream. There are many stiles and gates and, after some distance, the path reaches the farm buildings by Blackford Mill. Here, the waters race down the sluices as though they were eager to start the machinery working again!

Walk to the left in front of the farmhouse, then around the side of the mill to cross over the Alne and a stretch of waste ground to a stile leading to a school playing field. At the far side is the A3400 with Henley a few steps to the right.

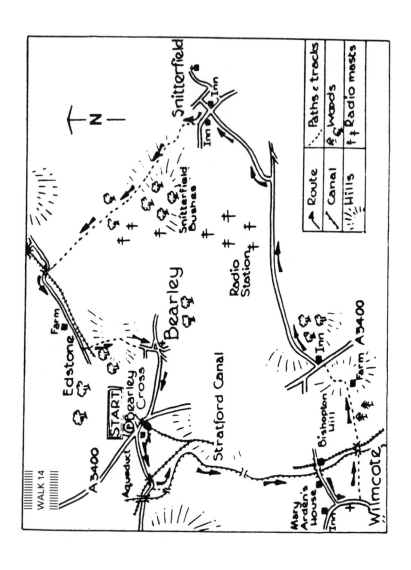

WILMCOTE AND SNITTERFIELD

WALK 14

★

10 miles (16 km)

OS Landranger 151

'. . . In spring time, the only pretty ring time,
When birds do sing, hey ding a ding, ding,
Sweet lovers love the spring.'

This is Shakespeare's England — and spring time is the best
season to wander over the hilly countryside and through the
wooded dells where the young Shakespeare roamed. The villages
abound with associations with the poet — legends of his boyhood,
poaching expeditions and family homes.

It is said that he who knows Arden has looked into the heart of
England; the greenwood tree may now be rarer but this is still a
delightful area. So I hope you finish this walk singing like the
Forester of Arden in *As You Like It* — 'This life is most jolly'.

The walk begins at Bearley Cross on the old Birmingham
turnpike road about five miles from Stratford-upon-Avon and
one may park in quiet roads off the A3400 at Bearley Cross.
There was once an actual cross here, probably marking the
boundary of a district. Turn off the A3400 beside the Golden
Cross inn, along a lane signposted to Little Alne (Map
151/172610).

Shortly, over to the right, can be seen a spectacular aqueduct
carrying the Stratford-upon-Avon Canal. Go under a railway
arch then immediately turn left and walk alongside a stone barn.
Proceed beside the hedge to the canal towpath and walk to the
left. The silence of this peaceful way is disturbed only by the cry of
the moorhens and the wings of ducks splashing the water as they
accelerate for take-off.

On reaching a roadbridge (167583), leave the canal and go
right to the village of Wilmcote. The beautifully restored house of
Mary Arden, on the right, was the home of Shakespeare's mother
and there is a museum of agricultural implements and other rural
bygones. Turn left by an hotel and go past the tiny church
dedicated to St Andrew, which was built in 1841.

By a speed de-restriction sign, continue left along a

49

macadamed track. Climb a stile and walk along a clear way to the right, behind farm buildings.

Go over the canal bridge and, where the path divides by a copse, keep to the left of the trees and walk near a farm to the top of Bishopton Hill. On reaching the A3400 road, turn left (183582).

Stay on the main highway for only a few yards, then proceed right by the Dun Cow inn, a hostelry reputed to be where Shakespeare cooked venison poached on Sir Thomas Lucy's estate.

Remain on the lane for about 1½ miles, then turn left along The Green to the village of Snitterfield which has further connections with the Bard for his father came from this hamlet and his uncle Henry is buried in the churchyard of the 14th century church.

Take the first road left and go up the hill, past the Snitterfield Arms. Just past Highfield Close there is a field path, (212600). Soon walk alongside a sports field, with a hedge and allotments on your left, and at the end of the field, go over metal railings and around the corner of the adjacent meadow to climb a rather elaborate stile.

Continue up the border of a field. At the top of the slope, go through a metal gate and walk with the hedge now on the right. This is a fine high path with extensive views over a patchwork countryside. Keep beside the hedge on your right through several fields. After a stile and railway sleeper bridge, which is under low electric wires, proceed to a stile at the top left-hand corner of a long field.

Over the stile, immediately bear right through a gate and continue along a path that meanders through a wood seemingly full of scampering rabbits. Ignore the first stile on your left. Out of the trees, go over a stile to a field and walk across to a stile. In the next pasture, continue on the same bearing with a hedge again on the right, to a road by a railway arch (193621).

Turn left and stay on the road for about half a mile. Just after a black and white farmhouse, walk left along a signed bridleway. Cross over the railway at Edstone and go through a gateway at the edge of a copse. Continue with a hedge on the left to a gate leading to a track to Bearley. By the little church of St Mary the Virgin, with two fragments of Norman doorways, turn right along the road back to the Cross.

ASTON CANTLOW

WALK 15

★

6½ miles (10.5 km)

OS Landranger 151

There can be few Warwickshire churches more beautiful than those at Wootton Wawen and Aston Cantlow which we visit on this ramble.

The church at Wootton Wawen, standing defiantly just off the busy highway, may be the oldest in the county and parts date from Saxon times. It has a massive battlemented tower and is crammed with many interesting features.

The little church at Aston Cantlow, snugly surrounded by trees, is where Mary Arden from Wilmcote married John Shakespeare from Snitterfield. Their son, William, was born in 1564.

Aston Cantlow is a fascinating place. Named after the Cantilupe family, who were great landowners from the time of the Norman Conquest, and ambitious, it is a good example of a town that did not make the grade.

In 1227, having established the right to hold a weekly market and annual fair in Aston Cantlow, William de Cantilupe assumed that the town would prosper. However, the competition from neighbouring places such as Henley-in-Arden and Bidford appears to have been too severe and trade did not develop.

Peter de Montford's market at Henley, established by charter at about the same time, succeeded while Aston Cantlow remained a sleepy little hamlet. There is nothing left of the Cantilupes' castle except small earthworks, but one can still see the well-restored guild house.

Park along the B4089 in Wootton Wawen or in the lay-by by the village store (if it is closed). The walk begins by following the footpath opposite the gateway to Wootton Wawen church (Map 151/153632). Go through a kissing gate, then across a meadow through another gate to the river Alne. Do not cross the river but follow a clear path to the right, never far from the tranquil waters — where you may see a heron. A stile is reached by a wire fence which surrounds a water works. Over a second stile, follow the river again to a meadow.

51

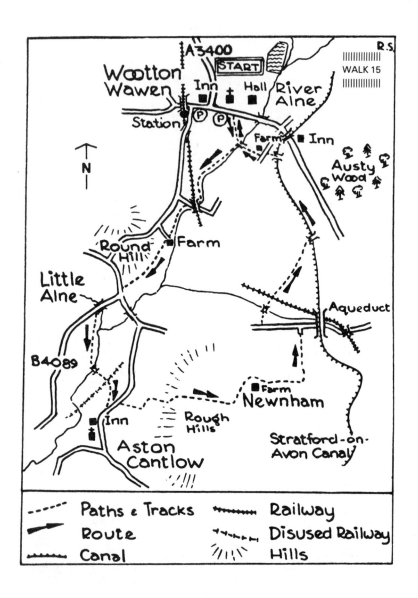

A 3400
R.S.
WALK 15
START
Wootton
Wawen
Inn   Hall   River
Alne
Station
Farm   Inn
Austy
Wood
N
Round
Hill
Farm
Little
Alne
Aqueduct
B4089
Farm
Newnham
Inn
Rough
Hills
Stratford-on-
Avon Canal
Aston
Cantlow

- - - -   Paths & Tracks   ┼┼┼┼   Railway
▬▶   Route   ┼╌╌┼   Disused Railway
╌╌╌╌   Canal   ⟋⟋⟋   Hills

Walk through the pasture to a railway bridge over a lane (140620). Go under the railway and along the lane for a few yards. Climb over a stile on the left and go on into a pasture bordering the river. Walk to the right of a red-roofed barn and climb over a stile into pasture land. Head to the right of a Georgian farmhouse and go through a white gate to a lane.

Cross straight over to a little concrete bridge, then over a stile. Veering to the left, climb Round Hill to a hunting gate about halfway along the opposite boundary.

Stay on the same heading over another pasture then cross a field to the left of some cottages. Climb a stile to a lane (142613). Turn left; then right at a road junction and pass some fine black and white houses.

Just after a small bridge with white railings, take a path on the left. Across the meadow, go over a stile and walk along a clear path to cross the river. Here there is a row of elegant willows and beyond you will see a kissing gate. Cross the old railway track to a stile. Veer right, across the field to a lane leading to Aston Cantlow.

From the village, take the Bearley Road to the left then turn right along a signposted field path (140602). The track now climbs the ridge of Rough Hills, the way bearing left as it goes up the steep slope. (This path, by the way, is termed by the council an 'unclassified road'.)

Proceed through a gate. The hedge is now on the left. Pass through a metal gate, and cross a sometimes cultivated field. At the edge of the field, our way bears sharp left, past an old hut. Follow the farm track to the hamlet of Newnham.

The lane leads to a road where there is a lofty aqueduct of the Stratford-upon-Avon Canal. Turn left. Just past the drive to Silesbourne Farm, look on the right for a stile (158608). Walk straight across the field.

Cross the abandoned railway track, then go over the brook by a railed bridge and into a pasture. Now aim for a crossing place of the railway track. Walk through an ancient orchard. Keep ahead — the direction over a fence is waymarked. Follow the line of the hedge on your right up the slope.

At the field boundary, go over the fence. Soon a new stile is reached and you go along the drive of a new bungalow. This brings you back to the canal again. Descend to the towpath and walk in a northerly direction to bridge No. 54.

Leave the waterway by turning left along a track in front of bungalows (156627). On a lane, walk left for a few yards. Go through a kissing gate which leads to a footbridge over the river Alne. Now turn right, along the original way back to Wootton Wawen.

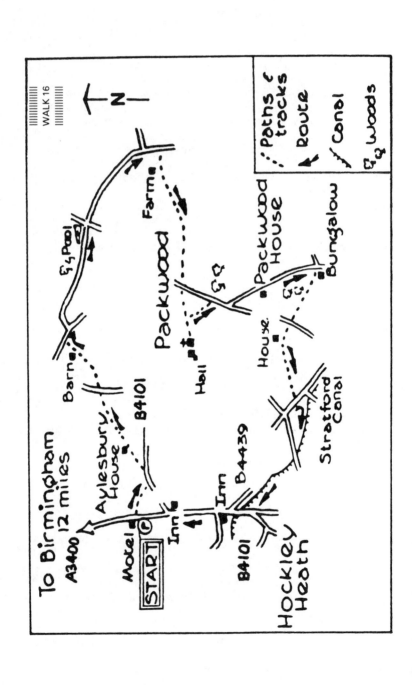

WALK 16

N

To Birmingham
A3400
12 miles

Motel

START ©

Inn

Aylesbury
House

B4101

Barn

&₃ Pool

Farm

Packwood

Hall

&₅

Packwood
House

&₆

House

Bungalow

Inn

B4439

B4101

Hockley
Heath

Stratford
Canal

Paths &
tracks

Route

Canal

&q Woods

PACKWOOD HOUSE

WALK 16

★

6 miles (9.5 km)

OS Landranger 139

Packwood House, the ancient seat of the Fetherston family, is approached down lanes little more than a dozen miles from the centre of Birmingham.

The present mansion dates from the 16th century but the owners over the years have much altered the place. However, the garden, planted by John Fetherston between 1669 and 1711, remains to be admired to this day; the clipped yews are said to depict the Sermon on the Mount. There are the multitudes, the Apostles and the large tree meant as Christ.

The house is now the property of the National Trust. From whichever direction the sun may beam, its rays are sure to be caught by one of the many decorative sundials; one dates from 1660 and another bears an inscription for the Latin scholar of 'Septem Sine Horis'.

Park in a lay-by near the starting point of the walk (see sketch map); it starts from the A3400 road at Hockley Heath. Just opposite a motel is a stile leading into a field (Map 139/152733). This stile lies well back from the road, between houses. Further stiles indicate the way to the B4101. Turn left.

A few yards along the main highway is a white kissing gate leading to a clear pathway which crosses the drive of an elegant old house, Aylesbury House (now an hotel). Climb a double stile and the track continues with a hedge on your left. Over a bridge and rivulet and by a little pool, veer away from the field boundary to pass a water trough to a road.

Proceed to the left, and soon there is a signed path on the opposite side of the road. We are in a huge field now but there is a good marker — the bridge on the far side. Over the stream, bear left to a stile. Beyond this is a ruined barn and a track over the pasture to a lane (168740). Turn right.

A little way on the left, walk along Mill Pool Lane — a narrow, lovely road, past old cottages. There is birdsong in the air.

We go by the pool, on the far side of which Darley Mill is demurely hidden under thick ivy. Go straight over a crossroads and take the lane towards Chessetts Wood. Just past Chapel Lane (which is on the left), we go right, along the drive of Chessetts Wood Farm, and nearing the farmhouse, we go through a metal gate to the left.

Veer to the right, so that you are now walking alongside a hedge. Follow the edge of a sometimes cultivated field to a plank bridge and a railing stile, then climb a pasture beside a wire fence. A gentle, agreeable landscape now — open and green.

After a stile, go across a fast-flowing brook; rather concealed here are a couple of old stiles. Continue through meadowland alongside a farm drive and with a hedge on your left, to arrive at a lane (174729). Cross to a kissing gate. We are now aiming towards the tower of Packwood church. St Giles' has a nave from the 13th century but whether there is any truth in the story that the tower was rebuilt by Nicholas Brome, like Baddesley, as a penance for a murder, we know not.

Near the church, to the west, is Packwood Hall. The farmhouse, still fully moated, was once the site of a residence for the prior and monks of Coventry. Retrace your steps towards the lane but, a short distance before this is reached, go over a stile on the right. Walk straight across a sheep pasture to a stile onto a road. Turn right.

Through the gateway, we are at the estate of Packwood House. Nearby are the fine stables which, dating from the time of John Fetherston, about the 1660s, are said to be more rewarding architecturally than the great house, no doubt because alterations over the centuries have been few.

Continue the ramble along the lane to the south. By the road turning to Chadwick End, go up a step-stile on the right. The pathway borders the garden of a bungalow and continues to the right of the garage. There is a wood on your right.

Climb over a stile and continue at the edge of a pasture and over a plank bridge. Another stile gives access to a field. Follow this around to a fence on the right. Climb this fence and walk over the parkland of Packwood to a lane. There is a fine view across the lake to the great house.

Cross the lane to the vehicle way (which is also a public footpath) to Malt House Farm. Follow the track past a pool to a fence, which has to be climbed. Turn to the left through fields to a track leading to the B4439 and turn left.

After about fifty yards, go along a track to a balance bridge spanning the Stratford-upon-Avon canal, a waterway which, in the summer, is busy with holiday craft. A pleasant walk along the towpath to the right brings the rambler back to Hockley Heath.

TANWORTH-IN-ARDEN AND MOCKLEY WOOD

WALK 17

★

6 miles or 4½ miles (10.5 or 7 km)

OS Landranger 139

The extensive parish of Tanworth (the addition of Arden is quite recent to mitigate confusion with Tamworth), once contained a great number of manor houses including Umberslade, Codbarrow, Clayhall, Sidenhall, Beetlesworth, Lodbroke, Cheswicke and Crewenhale.

Many sites are now merely designated on larger-scale maps by moats. The families of the de Mowbrays, the de Montforts, Beauchamps and Archers often seem to be interwoven in the intricate patterns of ownership of the manors.

The Archers of Umberslade have many monuments in Tanworth church. This lovely building, dedicated to St Mary Magdalene, dates from about 1300. The village, with its traditional green (complete with spreading chestnut tree), old hilltop church and inn, is pretty and unspoilt. Perhaps being distant from any main road has helped. The railway line through the parish, built by the GWR in 1908, also avoided the village.

Park around the green in Tanworth-in-Arden but please avoid blocking access. From the main street turn right along Vicarage Hill (Map 139/113705). A short distance along, by tall Scots pine trees, go over a stile on the right. In the field, gradually bear right to another stile onto a lane.

Cross straight over to the drive to Leasowes Farm. (Leasowes is a popular name for farmsteads in the Midlands and denotes meadow land.) As the drive sweeps sharp right to the farm buildings, continue ahead through woodland.

There is a pleasant green way towards the Palladian-style mansion of Umberslade Hall, now converted to luxury apartments.

On a lane (134713), turn right. By the park entrance can be seen the moat of the ancient manor of Codbarrow which must have been of some size — about 132 feet by 120 — and belonged, in turn, to the de Montforts and the Catesbys before being sold to the Archers at the time of James I.

57

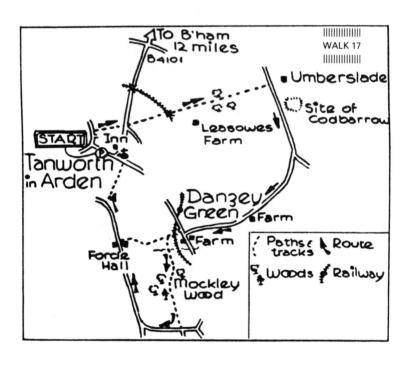

At a road junction, proceed to the right. We are now at some height and there are good views towards the south. The lane goes past Hill Farm, then descends to another road where , a yard or so to the right, is a farm track going over a railway (124694).

The way can be rather muddy. Walk through several gates and into a field. Here proceed sharp left to a ford across a stream. (If you prefer a shorter walk, once in the field keep straight ahead with a hedge on your right and follow the track around to Forde Hall.) Cross a meadow to Mockley Wood. Go through a gate and climb a slope which is covered with a carpet of bluebells in the springtime.

Follow the waymarked path to a hunting gate. Remain on the same heading through a field to a lane, where continue to the right. It is again right at a T-junction. We pass Forde Hall which obtained its name from one Roger de la Forde, who was granted the old manor house by John de Somery of Aspley at a rent of one shilling a year.

The lane climbs steeply out of the valley. Just over the brow of the hill go over a stile, on the right. A clear path leads us over pastures and then drops to a stile by a stream. The spire of the hilltop church of Tanworth acts as a beacon to lead the rambler back to the starting place.

After the walk, you can relax on the green conveniently near the inn!

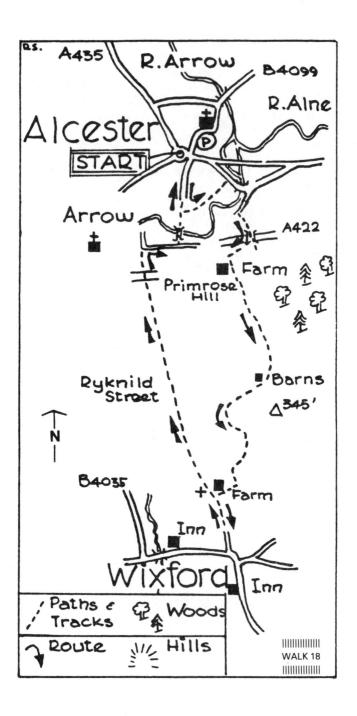

R.S.

A435

R.Arrow

B4099

R.Alne

Alcester

START

P

Arrow

A422

Primrose
Hill

Farm

Ryknild
Street

Barns

△345'

N

B4035

Farm

Inn

Wixford

Inn

Paths &
Tracks

Woods

Route

Hills

WALK 18

PRIMROSE HILL, WIXFORD AND ROMAN RYKNILD STREET

WALK 18

★

5½ miles (9 km)

OS Landranger 150

Excavations and discoveries in recent years have established that Alcester was founded as a settlement even before Roman times. It was the Roman occupation, however, which really established the town for it was situated on the old highway of Ryknild Street. The addition of buildings of different ages has created a delightful mixture of architectural styles over the years — black and white houses, mellowed stone and brick.

The town hall dates from 1618 and has stonework by the renowned Chipping Campden mason, Simon White. The church, dedicated to St Nicholas, is from the 13th century, but nothing remains of the old abbey.

The buildings of the town are maintained with great care and even unpretentious cottages are now being modernised with sensitive skill.

From the High Street in Alcester, where there is a car park, cross the Stratford Road to Bleachfield Street (Map 150/089573). Opposite a house numbered 95, go over a stile into pasture and continue with a hedge on your right. By some willow trees, enter the adjacent meadow, with the wire fence now on the left. Walk beside the placid waters of the river Arrow for a few yards then veer over to the left to the sports field and pass along the wing of a football pitch to the old Stratford Road.

Turn right and cross the ancient and beautifully proportioned Oversley Bridge, the arches of which have been here since 1600. Take the right-hand fork at a road junction and go along Mill Lane. Proceed left (Primrose Lane) by some cottages where the thatch dips low.

Walk over the bridge across the main road and climb the hill up the track to the right. Primrose Hill is a fine vantage point over Alcester town and the pastoral lands.

Just before the farm buildings, turn left along a farm track by some silos resembling space rockets! We are now in beautiful, rolling countryside where the only sound may be the persistent

61

note of a solitary skylark. After about half a mile the rough track goes 90 degrees right, through a gateway and past a green Dutch barn. There is from here a fine view across the valley to the stately Ragley Hall.

Walk along an avenue of laburnum trees to a Y-junction of tracks and continue left to the drive of Oversley Castle — a country mansion. Here, turn right, then left at a group of farm buildings to emerge on Ryknild Street (091549). A detour can now be made along this quiet way to the left to the hamlet of Wixford — termed 'Papist Wixford' in the rhyme describing Shakespeare's villages because the place was owned by the monks of Evesham Abbey. There are a couple of pleasant inns here.

Retrace your steps to the isolated church dedicated to St Milburgas which is situated on Ryknild Street. Although this church looks fascinating outside, it holds a magnificent treasure inside which many cathedrals would love to possess. This is the brasswork on the tomb of Thomas Crewe and his wife. Dating from the 15th century, the work is over nine feet long and beautifully preserved.

From the church, go along the sunken Roman road which now has the appearance of a playground for rabbits. Cross other tracks — the way now goes between hedges. Across the fields to the left is the little hill on which stood the original Oversley Castle, a wooden structure built by Ralph le Boteler in the 12th century, but nothing remains to be seen today.

Climb several stiles and stay on the same general heading. Soon Arrow Mill (now a restaurant) can be seen on the left. At the end of a field, go over the main road to Mill Lane. Beyond the main entrance to a caravan site, walk along a pathway to the left. Cross the river to reach Bleachfield Street again and so to Alcester.

PASTORAL COUNTRY AROUND ALVECHURCH

WALK 19

★

5 miles (8 km)

OS Landranger 139

Alvechurch was once the site of a moated summer palace for bishops; the reason why they selected this place for their holiday retreat 700 years ago seems to be lost in antiquity. All that remains now of the holiday home are a few earthworks near the river Arrow.

Today Alvechurch has much modern development but still retains an essentially village atmosphere with a grouping of old cottages and black and white buildings around the centre.

The church has a dedication to St Lawrence and the name of the village is thought to have been derived from the possible founder of the church, Aelfgytn (an Anglo-Saxon personal name).

The place of worship, on the traditional high lane, was largely rebuilt by an ardent Victorian restorer named Butterfield. He literally 'raised the roof' but the low 15th century tower escaped interference, so that the building now has a rather unbalanced appearance.

Around Alvechurch there are some fine pastoral lands in which we walk on this ramble.

From the car park in the village at Alvechurch, proceed along the main A441 road towards Redditch. After about a quarter of a mile, turn left through park-like gates (Map 139/030723). Keep on the main track over the river Arrow (which further downstream once powered many needle mills).

Soon after crossing the water, our pathway leads off to the right, as the main way bears left. Beyond the open fields walk past Newbourne Wood which is a reserve owned and managed by the Worcestershire Nature Conservation Trust.

Cross a road to Gravel Pit Lane — the road descends steeply to the valley — and on a sharp bend is the start of a signposted footpath by a white cottage. Go over a little brook and turn left. The pathway stays by the stream. After about half a mile and just before a lane, turn left to cross the brook by means of a

63

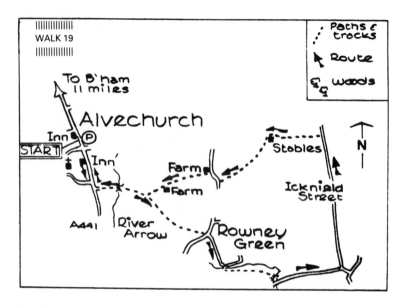

footbridge. A yard or two further along is a metal gate and the lane where you turn left. The quiet road leads to Icknield Street and our route is to the left (059713). This is the way the Roman legionaries travelled from the Fosse Way at Stow-on-the-Wold to their station at Wall, near Lichfield.

Stay on the Roman road for about a mile until you come to a white cottage on the left. Just beyond is a bridleway which goes through an attractive open landscape, then by a farm. Bearing around to the left, continue through the gateway and paddock of a riding establishment.

There are several more gates to be passed before a road is reached (045723). Walk to the right for a short distance to a metal gate which leads to Rowney Lodge Farm. A farm road goes over the hill to drop down to the vale of the Arrow and Alvechurch.

THE HILLS OF BIRMINGHAM

WALK 20

★

6½ or 2 miles (10.5 or 3 km)

OS Landranger 139

The Countryside Act empowered local authorities to create country parks to provide opportunities and facilities for enjoyment of open air recreation by the public. For many years there were plans to create such a park around the uplands of Waseley and Windmill Hills on Birmingham's doorstep to link the areas where, for many years, the public had had the right to roam. The Lickey Hills were opened to all when there was angry reaction to illegal encroachment and enclosure under the Act of 1803 which eliminated the former common-land. To the north, the Clent Hills are safe in the guardianship of the National Trust.

The designation of the Waseley Country Park has thus established a virtually unbroken band of green (or perhaps one should say 'yellow' some summers) countryside to the west of the city. The old image of a park as an amalgam of formal gardens, pools and trimmed lawns is soon dispelled; here is a place where nature is allowed to continue to weave its own patterns, and the grass is trimmed not by mechanical cutters but by grazing cattle.

The walk is in the shape of a figure of eight so that those folk who can only manage a short ramble can easily return to the starting place.

From the car park which has been provided below the rolling slopes of Windmill Hill by the Hereford and Worcester County Council (Map 139/972783), turn left along the narrow lane to Chapman's Hill.

By a farm, as the lane swings sharply to the right, continue along the rough vehicle track straight ahead. This way soon becomes a footpath through shaded dells and crosses the bed of a stream. Away up the hillside is Segbourne Coppice where the pool is an added attractive feature of the country park. But our way continues ahead — again the track can accommodate vehicles — past a house to another track by Chadwich Grange Farm (970771). The pathway which climbs the hill to the left is now our direction — the signpost says 'Rubery'. The views are very fine;

65

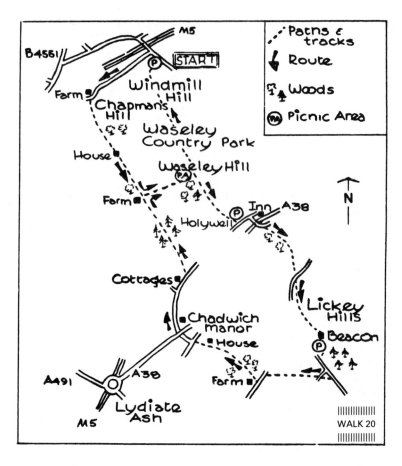

the motorway goes along the vale with the vehicles, from afar, looking like a continuous trail of ants.

At the top of the hill is a picnic area.

For those who require a shorter ramble, through the gateway the car park can be reached by turning left and walking along the tops of the hills.

For the longer walk the way is to the right. Pick up the line of small oak trees, then descend to the left to a new stile and track to the car park at Holywell. 'Holy wells' were, in far-off pagan days, the subject of intense veneration and worship for their inexhaustible outpourings of clear water. With the arrival of Christianity, the worship of springs was forbidden but the basic prayers were so intense that the Church transferred the tutelage of wells to saints.

Cross the dual carriageway A38 (there is an inn nearby), then immediately leave the road by going along a track on the right. The way, bordered by tall holly, leads to a lane. Cross to a path which stays by the road going uphill for some distance, then veers to the left along the ridge of Beacon Hill. Continue to the squat tower.

Beacon hills are plentiful in the land. Many date from the middle of the 16th century when the Tudors, concerned about an invasion from over the Channel, planned an early warning system across the country. Beacons were again thought of when Napoleon's armies were mustering. Queen Victoria's jubilees were further excuses to light hilltop fires — and they brightened the countryside yet again for the celebrations of our present Queen's Jubilee.

From the beacon site (where there is now a directional indicator), turn to the right and go through the car park to a road. Proceed to the left and, after a short distance, there is a stile and footpath sign on the right (987757).

A clear path crosses a field and drive, then further fields to a lane. Turn left to a signed bridleway to Chadwich. The track goes past farm buildings and through woodlands of exquisite beauty, where sunlight filters through high branches, and then through the garden of a house to a drive and road.

Walk a few yards left to Redhill Lane and go under a main highway. We are soon away from the noise of traffic and near Chadwich Manor, a brick mansion dating from the late 17th century. Just past a row of cottages, turn left along a farm drive (974764). Take care by woods to leave the farm drive by climbing the stile alongside. There is now a nice pathway through a copse where squirrels play at being Tarzan.

Out of the trees, enter a pasture and make sure you follow the line of the path which goes in the centre of the field to a stile to the right of the farm buildings. We now rejoin part of the outward route by walking along the path uphill to the right. This time, however, beyond the hilltop picnic site, proceed to the left.

Over pastureland, keep to the uplands until the starting point can be seen away on your right.

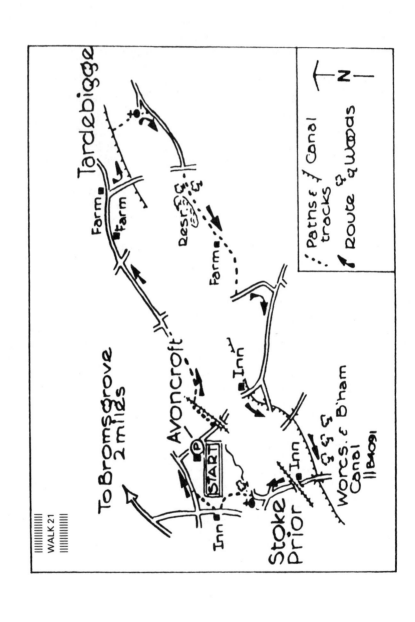

WALK 21

To Bromsgrove
2 miles

Tardebigge

Avoncroft

Stoke
Prior

Farm

Farm

Resr.

Farm

Farm

Inn

Inn

Inn

START

Worcs. & B'ham
Canal

B4091

N

Paths & Canal
tracks

Route of walks

AVONCROFT AND TARDEBIGGE

WALK 21

★

7 miles (11 km)

OS Landranger 139 and 150

In this age of change and demolition it is very pleasant to visit Avoncroft Museum of Buildings, near Bromsgrove, and see something of our heritage of architectural styles.

I think it a little sad that one can travel today to the other ends of the continent (or even, no doubt, to the other side of the earth) and find buildings looking the same clinically square boxes as in the centre of Birmingham. Nowadays, the skyscraper blocks of our English cities would look very much at home in Munich or Sydney or anywhere. Not so long ago, there was great contrast between constructions in the cities of neighbouring lands — compare Bruges and Amsterdam.

At Avoncroft, buildings removed from their original sites when threatened with destruction have been reconstructed on the attractive ten acre site. So we find structures from towns, such as an inn or a chairmaker's workshop, and a rural granary and windmill. The postmill was originally at Danzey Green near Tanworth, and was brought to Avoncroft in 1969. The internal machinery has been restored, so that the mill is a working building once more.

From the car park at Avoncroft go away from the main road and towards the railway arch (Map 139/960681). Just before the bridge, there is the start of a footpath on the left which goes beside the tracks for some distance. Continue to a bridge to cross the railway. In the field walk by a hedge to a gateway (no gate). Turn left. Keep the next hedge on your left to a vehicle track to a junction, then take the lane signposted to Tardebigge. Go over the crossing at Grimley Lane and by the ancient black and white Stonehouse Farm.

Opposite the farm and barns of Dusthouse go to the right along a narrow lane (988695). One might imagine we should descend to the Worcester and Birmingham Canal but, in fact, it is quite a sharp ascent. On the towpath, ensure you are now going in the corect direction.

Just past a lock-keeper's cottage, there is a stile on the right and a pathway over the meadows to the hilltop church of Tardebigge. This surely must be one of the most beautiful churches in the Midlands, with the most slender of spires — a lovely landmark. The original church collapsed in 1775 and this building was constructed the following year to a design of Hiorns, from Warwick. It was almost as though he wished to get right away from the fortress-like towers of that ancient city.

Near the church is the grand mansion of Hewell Grange where the Earls of Plymouth once lived but the present mansion at Hewell Grange, built in an Italian style during the last century, is now a Remand Centre.

Resuming the ramble, our next pathway goes at the side of the school, then by the playing field on the left to a stile onto a lane. Turn right. Past High House Farm there is a wide vista of a countryside tinted in yellow and brown. At London Lane, cross to the vehicle track opposite, which is a right of way for walkers. The way overlooks a reservoir used to top up the nearby canal. Completed in 1815, the canal climbs 220 feet in 2½ miles along this stretch and the top lock is said to be one of the deepest in the land.

Walk past Patchett's Farm and continue to a lane. Our way is now to the left, then right at a T-junction along Copyholt Lane. Cross Sugarbrook Lane to the canalside inn, the Queen's Head, the attractive inn-sign reminding us of Victoria's reign from 1837 to 1901. On the towpath go to the left, passing many locks, to Stoke Wharf which, in the 'Canal Age' was a busy commercial 'port'.

On the B4091 leave the waterway to go by the Navigation Inn and under the railway to Fish House Lane on the right. Hidden in the trees, beside an equally concealed meandering river Salwarpe, is Stoke Prior church. This is the area of salt and one of the windows in the church is a memorial to John Corbett who led a movement against the employment of women in the salt mines in the 19th century.

Within a few yards, leave Fish House Lane by going to the left along a vehicle track beside the white Stoke Meadow Cottage (951677). We cross the bubbling river where once, I should think, was a mill. The track climbs to the B4091 but we soon leave the road again by the second footpath on the right to cross the drive of Avoncroft College to reach another road. Turn right, then first right again brings us to the land of the windmill and the buildings of bygone ages.

THE HIGH MALVERN RIDGE

WALK 22

★

5 miles (8 km)

OS Landranger 150

When the 17th century diarist, John Evelyn, visited the British Camp perched high on the Malvern ridge, he recorded that it had 'one of the goodliest views in England'. This description still applies and the woods on the lower slopes of the hills are especially beautiful at all times of the year.

The camp, one of the most impressive earthworks in Britain, dates from the third century BC. When further fortifications were added before the Roman Conquest, it is thought that up to 20,000 people could be housed within the mile-long outer perimeter.

A plinth nearby records that, hereabouts, William Langland, a contemporary of Chaucer, 'slombred in a sleping' and dreamt his *Vision concerning Piers Plowman*, a long poem about the social conditions of the day.

From the car park (Map 150/763404) off the A449 near British Camp, 4 miles south of Great Malvern, follow the winding path up the steep slopes of Herefordshire Beacon. The unfolding views of the Herefordshire Hills and the Vale of Avon are a feast for the eye. On a clear day the Welsh uplands can be seen on the western horizon.

Those ancient Britons certainly knew where to site their vantage points. Up and up goes the path — then we attack the final earthwork and are on the breezy summit. One wonders for how long the ramparts can withstand erosion by thousands of visitors' feet.

But we must continue. Follow the way indicated on a directional sign to Hangman's Hill — where once stood a gibbet to teach sheep stealers a lesson. We pass Clutter's Cave or the Giant's Cave. One would like to report that romantic tales are woven around this hollow in the volcanic rock, but it would seem merely that it is named after a rather *small* shepherd who lived in the cave during the last century!

Drop down to the gulley on your right — there are direction indicators — and head towards woodlands. Soon the woods are

71

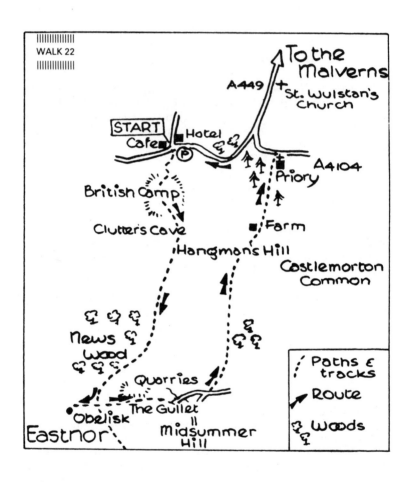

on the right and the high Malvern ridge to the left. The delightful path follows a way through the trees.

There is a high latchgate into Eastnor Park. The path leads to an obelisk, erected in 1812 by Lord Somers. The needle-like structure is a landmark for miles and was built of limestone instead of the hard local rock. Eastnor Castle, although looking every inch a Norman fortification, is a sham castle built by the first Earl Somers early in the 19th century.

Retrace your steps to the latchgate and park boundary and walk along the track by the Gullet Quarry. This place is well known to geologists who here study some of the oldest rocks in the land. The track has widened into a lane and, at a T-junction, turn left down a steep hill and cross a stream.

The next junction of roads follows very soon. Here leave the road and turn left — the way heads towards woodlands and bisects the green open pasture. Continue to the left-hand edge of a wood and keep ahead to pass the black and white Underhill Farm. We soon go by a most beautiful building, the former Benedictine Priory of Little Malvern. The original charter was granted in 1125 but much of the Priory was rebuilt from about 1480, only to be damaged at the Dissolution in the next century.

At the A4104, turn left to the A449, where another left turn takes us back to our starting place to complete the five mile walk A short diversion can be made to the little Roman Catholic church of St Wulstan, Little Malvern, where Sir Edward Elgar, who gained so much inspiration from his beloved Malvern Hills, lies buried in the churchyard.

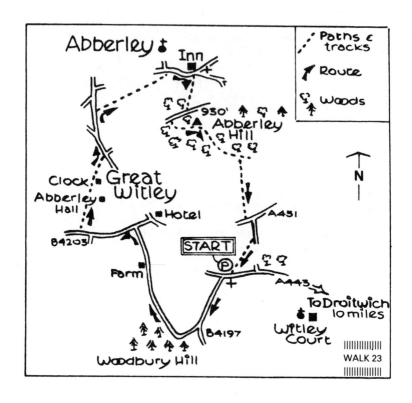

ABBERLEY HILLS AND
GREAT WITLEY

WALK 23

★

6½ miles (10.5 km)

OS Landranger 150

Situated some five miles south-west of Stourport, the Abberley Hills rise to almost 1,000 ft. The slopes are wooded and contain a maze of footpaths.

On a visit to this area, a look at Witley Court is well worth while. The large mansion dates partly from the 17th century. It was rebuilt on a grand scale in 1860 and gutted in a fire in 1937. However, the ruin is spectacular and the neighbouring St Michael's church, built in a European rather than English style, has beautiful interior decorations.

From the car park at the junction of the B4197 and A443 roads (Map 150/757657) walk about a half a mile along the B4197, then take the narrow lane on the right. The quiet way goes below the slopes of Woodbury Hill on the summit of which — hidden in the pine trees — are the earthworks of an ancient camp. It was to these heights that Owen Glendower came with his own countrymen aided by the French to do battle with Henry IV who was on the opposite Abberley Hill — although no battle ensued!

Go by the farm and oasthouses to the B4203. Turn left. Just beyond a road junction proceed through the gateway of Abberley Hall, now a residential school.

We pass Jones's Folly — which local folk call the clock tower. It resembles a country cousin of Big Ben; Mr Jones, who lived at the Hall, built it in memory of his father in 1883.

Continue along the wide track to the A443 (746670). Proceed to the left but soon leave the main highway by going along the B4202. After a few hundred yards there is a footpath on the right which leads straight to Abberley village and the Manor Inn.

Nearby is the tiny church dedicated to St Michael. The first church here was built when Offa ruled Mercia but this structure was replaced by the Normans; the local soft stone had been used and it was found necessary for the Lord of the Manor to build another church.

In 1963, dedicated volunteers lovingly restored the ancient

75

chapel and surrounded it with a tranquil garden.

The next path starts opposite the inn and is signposted to Wynniatts Way. Down the vehicle drive, look for a stile to climb by a garage on the left. In a field, keep approximately parallel to the drive to pass just to the right of a stable. Proceed with woods on your right to a stile. Climb through the trees to a lane.

Turn right to another path — signposted to 'Main route North'. The track snakes a way uphill to the trig. point at 930 feet.

From the trig. point, the path can be a little obscure at some seasons but I do not think you will stray if you retain the height when there is a choice of ways.

Stay on the heights of the hill for some distance until you reach the fifth WW sign after the trig. plinth. A path descends steeply to the right.

On the A451 (759663) continue to the left for a few yards, then turn along the lane on the opposite side of the road. Look for the start of a path on the right. This track leads diagonally across to a stile by the car park on the A443.

THE OLD FORESTS OF CHADDESLEY

WALK 24

5 or 2½ miles (8 or 4 km)

OS Landranger 139

It is often the unexpected that makes a ramble so interesting. On this walk I came, by chance, across a most beautiful nature reserve in Chaddesley Wood. It contains an outstanding example of lowland English oak-wood which is believed to be a remnant of an ancient forest. An additional feature of the woods is the Jubilee Walk, introduced in 1977 to mark the Queen's anniversary.

The paths through the woods are well waymarked and a delight. The starting place of the walk is Chaddesley Corbett, the main street of which has a varied collection of building styles with especially fine typical black and white Worcestershire work and Georgian fronts. The only church dedicated to St Cassian in England is here. It dates from the time of the Normans, although the tower and spire — a prominent landmark — are 18th century additions.

Park in one of the quiet streets of Chaddesley Corbett village. Opposite the Swan Inn a signposted path starts (Map 139/893737). Walk along a clear way then go over a stile, and along a farm track. A well walked way goes through fields to Chaddesley Woods.

Beyond a stile into the woods is a good waymarked path. Keep straight ahead, following the yellow signs. As you climb the steep slope, fine vistas over the Worcestershire countryside come into view. At a track, follow the directions indicated by the yellow arrows. This is a beautiful way through the ancient forest and the new plantations. At a junction of ways, turn right for the shorter walk. For the longer ramble, proceed a yard or so left. The Jubilee walk is waymarked white but we continue following the yellow arrows. Keep ahead up the incline when there is a junction.

Arriving at a Nature Conservancy signboard — check your position on the guide map nearby — climb a stile into a pasture (912733). Proceed with the woods on your left to a lane. Cross straight over to a stile back into woodlands — this time the Santery Hill Wood — and follow the boundary to a road.

Turn left for about a third of a mile to a bridleway, the sign by

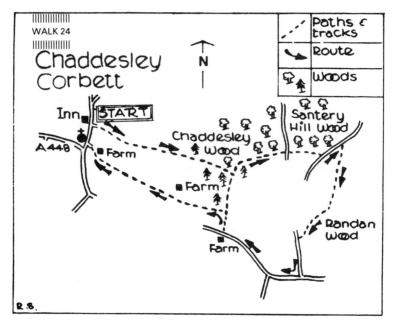

which shows the way to the right to Randan Wood. The track appears to be well used by horse riders and is rather boggy until it climbs to higher ground. Emerging from the trees at a sheep pasture, keep the wood on your right to stiles. These lead to the drive of Highwood Cottage. Continue to the right to a lane (916726), then turn left to the A448.

Proceed to the right for about three-quarters of a mile along the A448. Go right along the drive to Wood Farm (906725). Just before the wood, climb over a stile on the left, into a meadow. Stay on this same heading to walk through a field gate and a gap in the hedge to gain the top of the ridge. Over a hard track, keep a hedge on the left. This direction means you should see farm buildings straight ahead, beyond which is the village of Chaddesley Corbett.

THE CLENT UPLANDS

WALK 25

★

5½ miles (9 km)

OS Landranger 139

A guide published in 1868 recorded that 'those great clouds of smoke that darken the whole northern and eastern heavens during the prevalence of winds from those quarters, have stained the north and east sides of the trees on Clent Hill . . . you never see here a milk white sheep'. Today these uplands are carefully guarded by the National Trust, the air is clean and bracing and the views a tonic.

The hills form one of the great watersheds of central England: some of the waters flow westward to the Severn, others join the Trent and thence run into the North Sea.

The village of Clent has a brook tumbling over the pebbles alongside its street. The age of the church is deceptive as, although the tower dates from the 15th century, much of the rest was rebuilt during the last century.

We read that one of the incumbents was Parson Littleton Perry whose 'proceedings caused great scandal' after his institution in 1780. Whatever these proceedings might have been he nonetheless stayed in the living for thirty-seven years.

Park in the car park beyond the Vine inn at Clent. From the church, walk along the lane signposted to Walton Pool (Map 139/929794), look for a kissing gate on the left and the path to cut off a corner of the pasture to a lane. Proceed about a hundred yards along the drive opposite. Next to the white gates is another kissing gate and, across the meadow, a stile onto a road.

Cross to the stile opposite and walk over the field to bear right beyond the barn to a stile giving access to a farm track. Turn left.

There is now a steady climb to Calcot Hill where, in the 18th century, Richard de Caldcote, the lord of the manor, lived. (For a shortened ramble, you can turn left by the former farmhouse.) Our way is right. A vehicle drive goes through a filled quarry to a vehicle track by a house. Turn left to the road on Sling Common (947780) and continue to the left along Shutt Mill Lane. Alongside is a fast-flowing brook which once supplied the power to the steel grinding mills of Belbroughton.

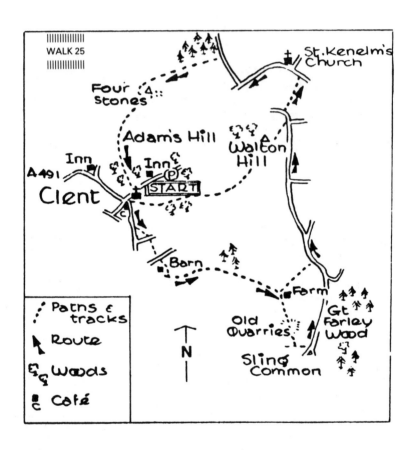

WALK 25

Four Stones

St.Kenelm's Church

Adam's Hill

Walton Hill

Inn

Inn

A491

Clent

START

Barn

Farm

Paths & tracks

Route

Woods

Café

Old Quarries

Gt Farley Wood

Sling Common

N

80

When the road divides, our way is to the left. There is now quite a climb to regain height. Over the brow of the hill are several tracks leading off to the left, which would take the rambler on a shortened route back to Clent. If you are still continuing, however, look for a signposted path (945802) on the right which crosses to St Kenelm's Road. The church is a short distance to the left.

This church, in 1974, celebrated its millenium — a thousand years of recorded history. The dedication of the church is due to the fact that the first building here was the place where Kenelm, the boy king of Mercia, was murdered in AD 973.

Continuing the ramble, stay on the lane and take the first turning to the right. After about a third of a mile there is a clear track on the left beside woodlands. This pathway climbs the hillside to the Four Stones, standing stones which look Druidical. In fact, they were dug from local quarries and set in place only about 200 years ago by Lord Lyttleton of Hagley as a decorative feature.

Soon bear left away from the horse gallops and walk through woodlands. The path now descends steeply to Clent village.

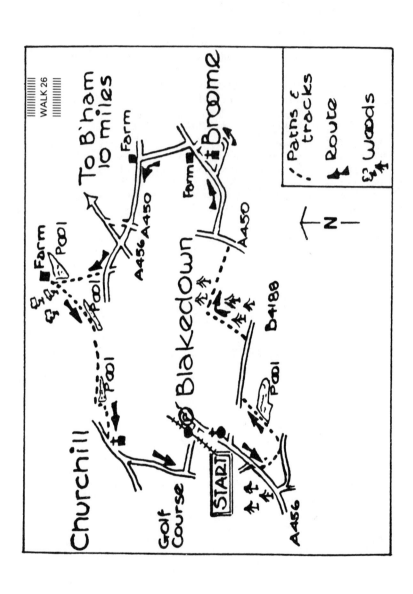

BLAKEDOWN AND
A VALLEY OF MILLPOOLS

WALK 26

★

5 miles (8 km)

OS Landranger 139

This is a walk of mills and millpools. At every twist and turn on the paths and lanes to the east of Kidderminster we see evidence of the great use made of the water power of quite humble streams and there is even one mill where the giant waterwheel still continually turns.

One of the villages we visit is Churchill. This is sometimes referred to as Churchill-in-Halfshire, the latter part of the name coming from the old hundred or judicial county division in which the place was situated. The place name is rather a puzzle as the Domesday Book calls it Cercehalle but does not record a church or priest here; the present church dates only from the 19th century and does not stand on a hill.

From the village of Blakedown where you can park in Station Drive, at the north end of the village, leave the main Kidderminster Road (A456) by turning down Halfshire Lane (Map 139/876782). The lane immediately bears sharp right but we keep straight on along a vehicle track. Over on the left is a lovely lily pond. Soon the track becomes a leafy bridleway.

At a lane turn left, but almost at once leave the tarmacadam again and walk along a path beside New Wood Farm. Keep alongside the hedge, the way now going over attractive undulating countryside to arrive at a wide pool. As I proceeded, keeping by the waterside, I watched the antics of a grebe as it plunged for long periods of time into the cool waters.

Cross a pasture to the B4188 (883783) and turn to the right for a few hundred yards. Look for a signposted path alongside a pine wood. Go through a hunting gate and keep by the trees for about half the distance along the woodland. There is then a stile in the hedge on the right and a track going at right-angles to our former path. The way goes straight to the A450 road (895784) where turn left to the turning to Broome.

This hamlet was once surrounded by heathland and lay within the ancient limits of the vast Feckenham Forest.

The tiny brick church dedicated to St Peter is a gem. It is not old, for it was constructed in the last century, but it looks very continental and would be at home towering above Italian villas. An ancient bell, which was removed from the tower in 1945, hangs in the trim churchyard.

Beyond the church, the road bends round to the left. (There are more houses of great charm — although, unfortunately, the village seems to lack an inn or a store.) Walk to the right at Broome Farm, then take the first turning left. A quiet way goes to a T-junction where turn left to cross the A450 and A456 highways. About a quarter of a mile further, turn right along the drive of Brake Mill Farm — a bridleway and right of way for walkers (893796).

A fine track goes by another pool — you will see many millstones about as a reminder of a bygone era. By a farm, bear sharp left along a way bearing a notice 'Fir Lodge' and then, after a short distance, a footpath leaves the drive and goes to the edge of a wood.

By more areas of water, we reach a lane. We only keep on this for a little way to the right — there is another field path sign directing us over a stile. When a pool is reached, turn left into a most beautiful and peaceful spot where the waters tumble onto the blades of a wheel. Past the pool, veer right along a vehicle track. Almost immediately take a footpath and, going over a stile, follow the line of the stream to a road.

We go to the left and soon return to Blakedown. (There is something soothing about water, so away with the tranquillisers for a day and try this ramble as a medicine!)

KINVER EDGE

WALK 27

★

3½ miles (5.5 km)

OS Landranger 138

Kinver is now away from the main roads. However, the village was formerly of some importance as a resting place for pack horses on the great road from Chester to Bristol and many inns were provided with extensive stables.

Today, it is the great, red sandstone ridge which brings visitors to Kinver. The Edge has extensive earthworks and entrenchments, the origin of which is open to debate but they have been attributed variously to Ancient Britons, the Mercian King Wulfere and the Danish invaders. The ridge was afforested by Henry II.

The place name is Saxon and means a 'great ridge' or 'the ridge of the king'.

About 100 years ago, folk were living in rock excavations along Kinver Edge. Holy Austin Rock, a medieval hermitage, was used as a rock house. A contemporary writer stated that the people were 'thoroughly satisfied with their position in the world and, although many of them were begrimed with smoke, not one would have exchanged positions with the most eligibly located individual in Her Majesty's dominions'.

Now there is little smoke to mar the vistas across the vale to the distant Clee Hills.

You can park at the end of Church Road in Kinver and the walk starts near the National Trust signpost (Map 138/838828). Walk to the right of the edge of a large area of grass by a house and aim towards a clump of oak trees. Nearby is a stone plinth which informs us that 'at a meeting held on the spot on the 29th September, 1917, about 200 acres of Kinver Edge were given to the National Trust as a memorial to Thomas Grosvenor Lee and Winifred Hannah Lee'.

Veering left, go up the slope with tracts of heather and gorse to the left, a colourful sight during late summer, while in the far distance to the south can be seen the heights of the Abberley Hills and the serrated ridge of the Malverns.

Soon the pebbly track bears left and we have reached the steep

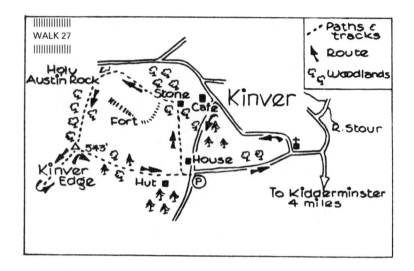

scarp slope of Kinver Edge; here we can stay awhile and let the eye rest on the lovely views over the rich farmlands of the river Severn stretched like a patchwork cover below our feet.

The pathway hugs the plateau of the Edge past the triangulation plinth which is at a height of 543 feet. You can, if you wish, continue for a distance before retracing your steps to the trig. point. There is now a wide path to be taken through the heather, going away from the escarpment. Through woodlands of small oaks, then tall conifers, the track descends to an area of grass. Nearby is a wooden shelter.

Proceed to our starting place and cross to Church Road which leads to Kinver church. The building dates from the 14th century and the local red sandstone shows the signs of deep weathering over the years. A charter was granted by Charles I in 1627 to absolve the people of the village from the payment of taxes and doubtless the inhabitants wish this was still in force today.

It is a deep descent down Church Hill. Below is the village of Kinver and the valley which contains both the river Stour and the Staffordshire and Worcestershire Canal. (The canal is over 200 years old and was engineered by James Brindley.)

At the road junction (near a café) turn left to complete the ramble.

BEWDLEY AND
THE WYRE FOREST

WALK 28

★

8 miles (13 km)

OS Landranger 138

Bewdley, from the French for 'beautiful place', was once an important trading centre for goods carried up the Severn from the sea. The merchants sent their goods from Bristol in barges and grew rich on the proceeds. Elegant premises were built along the bustling waterside and the town has finely-proportioned buildings dating from the 17th and 18th centuries. The Georgian parish church, on an island site in the wide Load Street, was built in the prosperous times when the town was an inland port.

However, when James Brindley built the Staffordshire and Worcestershire Canal in 1771, Bewdley committed commercial suicide by rejecting the waterway. The canal was therefore dug along the Stour valley and the new inland port of Stourport was born. The resultant trading decline of Bewdley meant that industry by-passed the town in the 19th century, but many ancient attractive features remain.

One of the most interesting buildings is the Shambles. Situated in Load Street, the former butchers' market now houses a fascinating folk museum. The policy of the Museum Trust is 'to stimulate and maintain an interest in the history of the town and the natural history of the countryside around it'.

Before you start walking to explore the beautiful Wyre Forest, do allow time to explore the town of Bewdley, and especially the Shambles Museum.

There is a car park by the river Severn in Bewdley. From the noble three-arch bridge, built to a design of Telford and which had a toll house until it was destroyed to aid motor cars, walk along the riverside street upstream (Map 138/786754). The way becomes a path and we pass perpetually optimistic anglers. Soon we reach a place where the tall stanchions of an abandoned railway line remain in the middle of the river, like sentinels guarding the valley, grandiose structures which have a weathered attractiveness in this setting.

The track crosses a metal footbridge where the Dowles Brook

87

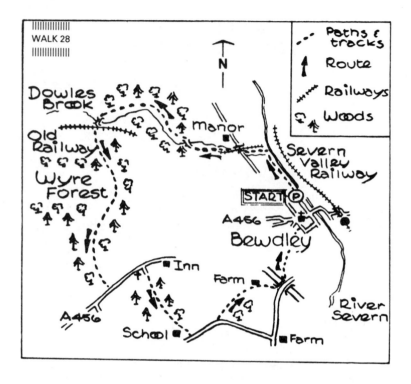

joins the main river. Here turn left, away from the Severn on a pathway which leads through the trees to the B4194. Turn right past the former bridge and immediately proceed left beside Dowles Manor, an Elizabethan residence snugly surrounded by woodlands.

A fine path stays not far from the Dowles Brook. (The name is probably Saxon — dowlas, meaning dark — but this seems a misnomer, for the water always looks clear and sparkling.)

At Oak Cottage is a bridge to cross the stream again and we pass a restored mill building in a picturesque setting. Continue to another bridge where we go over the brook (755767) before climbing the slope away from the stream and walking through gateways to cross the old railway route.

A clear pathway leads through Shelf Held Coppice to a clearing where the trees are replaced by pastures. Here, turn right (so that the field is on your left).

The way gradually veers around to the left; stay on the main path to emerge from the woodlands on a hard track over a cattle grid and a drive to a house. Continue to the A456 (757742).

A short distance to the left, on the opposite side of the road, is a lane, a right of way for walkers.

When the woodlands start, go along a wide track on the left — a bungalow should now be to your right. Keep along this track until you reach a gate to school grounds. Now continue (with a school to your right) along a vehicle track to a lane and turn left.

Stay on the lane until there is a sharp bend to the right (772738) when you walk through a wide gap in the hedge on the left and continue so that extensive woodlands are on your right-hand side.

When the trees end, climb over a stile and keep in the same direction bordering the hedge. Beyond another stile, the path goes by a copse and continues over the field to a stile in the small pasture attached to Park Farm. Proceed to the farm drive, turn right and climb the hill to a lane.

Our way is now to the left. After about 200 yards, look for the start of a footpath on the left. Go a few steps along a fenced way. Over one stile to pasture land, and then another, walk along a clear pathway.

High on the opposite ridge can be seen the mansion of Tickenhill. Here was a settlement in prehistoric times; then the Romans set up house. After the Normans, royal princes favoured the site, as did the Royalist forces during the Civil War.

Our pathway is now joined by a stream bubbling its way down the steep slope to Bewdley.

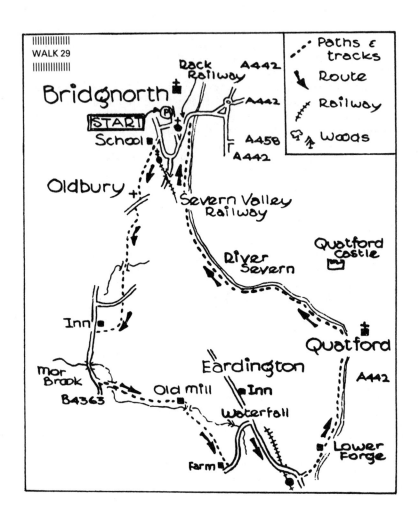

WALK 29

Paths & tracks

Route

Railway

Woods

Bridgnorth

START

School

Dack Railway

A442

A442

A458

A442

Oldbury

Severn Valley Railway

River Severn

Quatford Castle

Inn

Mor Brook

B4363

Old mill

Eardington

Inn

Waterfall

Quatford

A442

Lower Forge

Farm

BRIDGNORTH AND
THE VALE OF SEVERN

WALK 29

★

6½ miles (10.5 km)

OS Landranger 138

In the middle of the 17th century Thomas Fuller wrote about Shropshire thus: 'A large and lovely county, generally fair and fruitful, affording grasse, grain and all things necessary for man's maintenance, but chiefly abounding in natural commodities'.

I think everything today still tallies with Fuller's description.

This ramble can start by exploring that most spectacularly sited town of Bridgnorth. In England, in contrast to the continent, we seldom build our towns on hilltops. This is what makes Bridgnorth so rare.

The skyline is impressive; the ruin of the castle has a wall leaning at a very acute angle for it was damaged during a violent Civil War battle; the church with its domed tower was designed by Thomas Telford, the great engineer — and can any other inland town in the land boast such an exciting approach as the cliff railway ('open every day of the year')?

There are car parks in Bridgnorth and street-parking is allowed on Sundays. From the ancient town hall, which obstinately stands in the middle of the main street, turn into St Mary's Street.

At the main road (Map 138/715929), go a few yards to the left. Opposite Railway Street, leave the road by going along a rough vehicle way to the right signed by a footpath notice and 'SVR', initials standing for the Severn Valley Railway. It is here that the line starts, its lovely steam locomotives having been meticulously rebuilt by enthusiasts.

At the end of the vehicle way is a rather concealed gap on the right. Climb a fenced way and stile to a sports field. Aim to the left of the school to climb another stile. Cross a main road over the footbridge. Turn left then right. Cross a meadow.

At the B4363, we reach the hamlet of Oldbury where the tiny Victorian church is dedicated to St Nicholas. Turn to the right for one or two steps; you will then see a stile on the opposite side of the road beside a footpath notice, sadly lacking its arm.

By the line of a former hedge, now marked by a row of trees

and bushes, proceed sharp right to a stile leading to a sometimes ploughed field. Keep on the same heading to a bridge. This crosses a tiny stream which tumbles merrily down waterfalls and through a spinney; a pretty spot. Walk over another field to a lane at Coomsley (710911).

Almost opposite is a step stile and the start of a footpath. Stay by the left-hand hedge then keep ahead to go in front of a little white cottage. Beyond, enter a meadow and proceed right, then over a stile to a farm track and a road. Nearby is an inn.

Our way is now left to descend to the valley of the Mor Brook where the waters rush deep below the road. Leave the highway after 400 yards by going to the left along a bridleway into some attractive woodlands. By a field gate go into pastureland and keep to the edge of the trees and soon re-enter the woods.

Stay not far from the brook and reach a large mill. This building has fallen into a bad state and is, unfortunately, beyond repair. Cross the stream and walk away from the brook. It is very muddy here at all seasons but we soon reach drier land where there are Christmas trees first to the left, then to the right, of the path.

Continue past a hidden pool to the right amid trees. Take care here as the path is almost 'lost' at times. Keep ahead along the main track. You come to a stile adjoining a field gate. In the pasture go along the right-hand boundary and just before a long barn, go through a gateway on the left to a stile onto a road at the left of some cottages.

Proceed to the left. A lovely lane drops down to cross the brook again, by a noisy waterfall.

We are now at Eardington, once a centre for ironmaking. Little trace remains now except a ruin or two and the names of Upper and Lower Forges. At a T-junction, proceed to the right and cross the Severn Valley Railway. Opposite the station, go along a vehicle track to the left to reach the river by a nice row of cottages.

Follow the Severn upstream, over stiles and through meadows. On the opposite side of the river is Quatford. The Danes set up their camp on the strategic high ground here and the presence of the Normans is evident in the church. The story goes that Adelina, the wife of Roger de Montgomery, had a stormy voyage across the Channel and Roger vowed he would build a church on the spot where he met Adelina after her safe arrival. So the church on the sandstone rock at Quatford was founded.

Further along the river is Quatford Castle, a castellated mansion built by John Smalman as recently as 1830.

A few more meanders of the river and we reach the bridge of Bridgnorth, with the prospect of an easy climb up the cliffs to the town — on the railway!

CARDING MILL VALLEY AND THE LONG MYND

WALK 30

★

8 miles (13 km)

OS Landranger 137

It is not surprising that Church Stretton attracts those seeking a town for retirement; here there is beauty at all seasons of the year with the surrounding high hills constantly changing colour as though reflecting the many moods of Nature. To the east is a row of craggy outcrops, ruled over by the heights of Caer Caradoc, pre-Cambrian rocks and some of the most ancient in the land.

The other flank of Church Stretton is overshadowed by the great hulk of the Long Mynd which rises from the plain to a plateau over 1,600 feet above sea level.

From the top, small streams tumble and chase along little valleys (although here a valley is called a 'hollow' or 'batch'), and gleefully join with other brooks to the vale below.

The old houses are in the other Strettons — All Stretton, a village of black and white cottages and a manor house, and Little Stretton. Church Stretton's expansion came in the reign of Queen Victoria but the church shows its age with buttressed walls and doorways built by the Normans.

These hills are certainly invigorating but chronicles published soon after the turn of the century stated that the climate of the area 'is a tonic and has the valuable quality of exercising a somewhat tranquillizing influence on the nervous system and circulation'.

The ramble starts at the car park by the café and National Trust shop in the Carding Mill Valley a mile to the north west of Church Stretton. (Alternatively, the car could be left in the free car park in the centre of the town.) Go along a track, which climbs above the twisting stream as though heading back towards Church Stretton (Map 137/443944).

At a road, alongside a cattle grid, cross to a path signed to Town Brow. A copse, over to the left, contains a marked nature trail.

By a little reservoir our path turns left over the bridge and climbs sharply. Just over the brow of the hill there is a stile and path leading to a lane on the left. Turn right. The lane soon

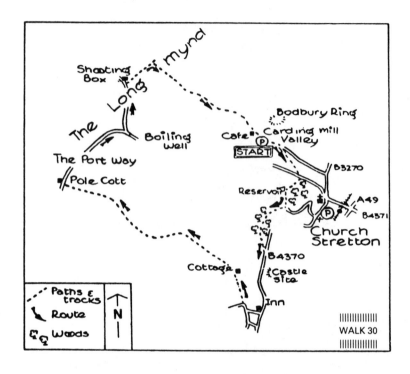

becomes a footpath through beech woods and joins the B4370, where turn right. Across the fields the earthwork of a castle can be seen in the trees.

At Little Stretton, turn to the right by the Ragleth Inn (443919) and right again near a black and white house. We now reach a ford; cross the stream and climb a stile into a pasture, follow the water upstream and go over more stiles.

By a rather isolated house we enter the extensive National Trust land of the Mynd at the entrance to the lovely valley of Ashes Hollow. The hills contract the valley almost into a gorge and the little brook, once powerful and scouring, now meanders through the sheep-clipped turf.

Soon the path becomes more rocky and makes an exciting clamber, high above the water. At a confluence of streams, our way is to the left. The valley meets another and at this point we cross the stream and veer to the left, pass a boggy spring and shortly afterwards reach the top of the ridge at the medieval track known as the Port Way.

Turn right (413938) and stay on the lane to a junction at Boiling Well, where proceed to the left.

94

After three-quarters of a mile take the sandy way to the right marked High Park at a shooting box where there are very fine views of all the Shropshire Hills, from the Wrekin to Wenlock Edge and the Clees.

Remain on the wide track until a point reached shortly after passing a pool and here turn right. There are many tracks and sheepways but aim for a deep gully. A little brook is a good marker. Soon a path will be seen, going down a steep valley, while on the summit of the hill ahead you will observe the earthwork of Bodbury Ring, a most commanding position for a prehistoric fortress.

The stream joins others and flows through the Carding Mill Valley, our starting place.